FROM ORPHAN TO MILLIONAIRE

BIG STEVE PROHASKA

For Chuck and Ellen Prohaska

CONTENTS

PROLOGUE

A few days ago, I was parked near the bus stop where my son Julian is let off after school, waiting for him to come running out to me, a daily ritual that is as important to me as anything in my life. No matter what's going on, I make sure I'm there to pick up my son as soon as those doors swing open; it's just something I promised myself I would always do. On this particular day, as he got into the car, I could tell there was something he was excited to tell me. A good grade, a funny story, taco day in the cafeteria - the usual stuff, the stuff that can make your day as a parent. "What's up, kid?", I asked with a smile. "There's a new kid at school. His name's Juan. He told us he came from Colombia. Didn't you say you were born there?"

The smile faded. I forced a response, "That's right,

you got a good memory," but something was activated inside me. The memories, the pain, the lives lost, the innocence that was violently taken from me. At 42, 35 years since I had last lived there, the simple mention of my home country is still enough to transport me to that distant time and place, to fill my heart with the sadness and loss that I experienced as a child in Colombia. I tried to keep cool as the images flashed in my mind - gunshots, dead bodies, the tears, the blood - but my son, observative like his father, knew something was wrong. "What's your deal, dad? You're acting weird." No bullshit, straight to the point, another thing he got from me. In our house, we communicate, we're open, we don't hide things from each other. At least, that's what I preach. In that moment, I realized that I never told him the whole story. He knew some of it - that I was an orphan in Cali, that I had been adopted and shipped to Connecticut, to live a strange new life in a strange new place - but not everything.

As we pulled into the driveway and Julian peppered me with questions, I was forced to face the prospect of telling my two sons the ugly, blood-stained truth. Were they old enough? Where would I begin? Julian knew I was hiding something, but maybe I could put it off, buy him a new video game to distract him. I didn't want to ruin that beautiful day with such a sad story, with a trip to the distant past full of nothing but pain. I opened the front door, and the first thing I saw was my beloved sneaker collection. The Bred 3's, Concord 11's, the OG banned 1's. My mother used to jokingly call my sneaker obsession a fetish; she didn't realize the reason I was so drawn to them was because there was a time I didn't have shoes, when I walked bare-footed across the hot, lifeless dirt of the courtyard at the orphanage. Usually my Jordans are enough to put a smile on my face, but today they were a beacon of hope, a symbol of how far I had come.

I looked around at the life I had built for myself. Two beautiful boys, my own house, the cars, the businesses, the experiences I can pass down to them and, someday, their kids. As tears welled in my eyes, I realized that despite difficult beginnings, my story isn't a sad one. It is a story of perseverance, of accomplishment, a story of a life truly lived and everything that comes with it. It was then that I knew I had to write this book. For my children, for my grandchildren, and for you and yours. I hope that it can serve as a symbol of hope, like my Jordans were for me.

One final word: There is very little remaining information documenting the earliest years of my life. All photos, journals, official documents, anything that I might use to reference that time, were burned to ashes when I was only five years old. There is no one to reminisce with, no one that can tell me stories about the day I was born, about the joy felt by grandparents that I don't remember. You might say my childhood itself was lost to time on the day my world was irreversibly, violently altered by Los Caballeros de Cali - the Gentlemen of Cali. So I ask that you bear with me and the haze of my early memories as I begin to tell you the story of my journey - from orphan to millionaire.

FROM ORPHAN TO MILLIONAIRE

BY BIG STEVE PROHASKA

CHAPTER 1

In Cali, Colombia, the Farallones de Cali cast a shadow over the city as the Sun burns into the Pacific Ocean on the Western horizon. It is under the cover of this shadow that the Cali Cartel operated from 1977-1993, when it became one of the most notorious and powerful drug trafficking organizations in history. At its height, yearly profits are estimated to have been as much as $7 billion. As fate would have it, it was also in this shadow that I was born, on January 2nd, 1981 - though this is only an estimate. The truth is, I may never know my real birthday.

I don't remember my parent's names. I don't remember the names of my brothers and sisters, even the two brothers I shared a bedroom with during those first five years of my life. I can barely remember my birth name, John, which my mother changed to Stephen shortly before her death. But I remember we lived in a small apartment on the first floor of a building somewhere in the heart of the city. As I think back, I can see the cramped kitchen with windows looking out onto the street, with a door that friends from the neighborhood would drive up to on their scooters. I can see my mother at the stove, always in an apron, her pale skin and long dark hair hanging over big pots of rice and beans, and I can see my father there, pacing, with his thick mustache, white polo shirts and cropped dark hair; he looked like El Chapo in the Netflix show, and something always seemed to be troubling him. I don't remember much about my father - I know that he was a laborer and didn't make much money. And I know that he had a brother that always seemed to be visiting - this was my uncle, the only extended family member I have any memory of. My uncle the drug mule.

The Cali Cartel was formed in 1977 when a group of kidnappers known as "Las Chemas" hit the jackpot, receiving $700,000 in ransom money in exchange for two Swiss citizens. This money was used to fund their drug trafficking empire, beginning with marijuana and soon shifting its focus to the more lucrative business of cocaine, which was exploding in popularity at the time. In those early days, the Cali Cartel was intimately linked with Pablo Escobar's Medellin Cartel and they, along with the other cartels that dotted the country, revolutionized the industry, introducing cutting edge innovations in production and distribution that took their drug from farms in Peru and Bolivia to the bloodstreams of people across the globe. Back then, the cocaine business was like free money, and there was plenty to go around as the recreational use of the drug skyrocketed around the globe. But the true cost of the trafficking business was hidden from the wealthy, glamorous users in Europe and the United States. They didn't know then that every line was paid for in blood.

Violence, and more commonly the simple threat of it, is one of the most vital tools used in the formation and management of any successful criminal enterprise. In Cali, the threat of violence hung over the city like the Farallones' shadow, from city hall to the ramshackle homes occupied by its many inhabitants. Violence was used to keep politicians in check, and was a deterrent against the many rank-and-file members of the Cartel speaking to authorities or stepping out of line. Low-level employees of the Cartel were often killed for mistakes, which served as a warning for others. But it was not the threat of violence against these footsoldiers that served as the greatest deterrent - anyone that got involved with the

Cartel knew the risk and accepted that each morning, when they left their homes and said goodbye to their wives and children, they may never return. It was violence against those family members themselves that acted as the most effective weapon in the Cartel's arsenal, the threat of the unthinkable that filled the air of the city like a noxious gas and ensured everything ran smoothly.

The many tentacles of violence and misery that extended from the power center of the Cartel reached into the homes of countless people in Colombia, including my own. My father himself was not involved - he was a humble laborer - and though drug mules are low on the trafficking totem pole, they make far more than a laborer, and it is my understanding that my uncle helped support our extended family through his work for the Cartel. Even as he took advantage of the financial benefits, my father worried about his brother - "Be careful, don't get killed, watch your back," I remember him saying during their frequent conversations at the kitchen table, conversations that often escalated into full blown arguments, always culminating in my father standing up and shouting, "No mas! No mas!" No more, enough.

Eventually, my father began to insist that my uncle separate himself from the Cartel, believing that the risk was not worth the reward. This was strictly forbidden - a man does not quit the Cartel like any other job - and it was understood that turning his back on the Cartel would put the lives of everyone in the family at risk. Still, my father pushed, and pushed, what seemed like every day as they sat there at the kitchen table while my siblings and I played and my mother cooked. "Que tu quiere?" my uncle would respond. "What do you want? What am I supposed to do? How will we get away? What will we do for money?" My father didn't have the answers, but it went on like this for some time.

Though I was only five years old, I was an observative kid, and at a certain point I noticed that a darkness had entered our home, a certain fear. My mother and father were talking more, serious conversations I heard only pieces of, always in the kitchen, by the stove, my mother in that apron, their pained expressions burned so clearly into my memory. "What's wrong, papa?" I would ask. "Don't worry about it," he'd reply, and my older sister would scold me and tell me to mind my business. When you're a kid, you don't know details, but you know something is wrong. Looking back, I understand now that a decision had been made. My uncle was going to leave the Cartel, and he and my parents were planning an escape.

This is no easy feat. You can't just move to the next

town over - they will do everything in their power to find you and make you pay to send a crucial message, one that is etched into their business model. Without the threat of brutality, what power do they have? To truly escape would mean leaving without a trace, the changing of identities, sneaking out of the country, immigration to the United States. And these things cost money, money we didn't have, even with the income brought in by my uncle's illegal activities. I can hear my mother's voice now, echoing in my mind. "Do you want me to sell my body? Do you want me to sell drugs? What can I do?" My father would stand there, hands on his hips, thinking. They knew what might be coming for them, for their children. They knew what might be coming for me.

Precautions were taken. We began changing locations, sleeping in the homes of people whose names and relation to our family I don't remember. I was taken to and from school at unusual times. I didn't understand it then, but I realize now that these were attempts to throw the Cartel off, so that when they did come looking for us they would receive contradicting information from neighbors, friends and teachers. It just might give us that smallest of windows through which we could find freedom. Strange men would ride their Vespa scooters up to our front door, not an unusual site in the streets of Cali where the homes let right out onto the streets - there were no driveways there - but these men walked right in and began talking to my mother as if they knew her, though I knew they didn't. They would ask for my uncle and my mother would play dumb. I believe now that this was the moment my uncle had begun the process of separating from the Cartel. Inevitably they would discover the truth. All we could hope is that we would be long gone by then.

My memories from this time are hazy. It was a long time ago, after all, and I was very young. The moving around, my parents' pained, anxious conversations, the men on Vespas, the palpable fear that had gripped our home - I'm not sure how long it lasted. Thinking back, it makes more sense that it would have been only a few days, though it felt much longer then. At some point within that period, my name was changed from John to Steven, the name I have used ever since. But the day that version of me, the day "John" truly died was one that I remember with absolute clarity, as if it is burned into my very soul, as if it is happening right here, right now in front of me as I write this.

I arrived home one day and saw that all of our things were packed. My mother was in a panicked hurry, ordering my siblings and I to make sure nothing important had been left behind. To my memory, my father was not there with us, only my mother, who stood in the kitchen burning what remained of our family photographs. This was so that the Cartel would not be able to identify us, so they wouldn't know who they were looking for or how many of us there were. This may seem drastic, but I know now that this saved my life. We scrambled as my mother's panic began to infect the rest of us. Then, I heard the sound of tires screeching to a halt.

It all happened in a flash. The first thing I saw was one pickup truck, a black Toyota like they had in *Back to the Future*, on the street outside my kitchen. Two guys in the cab, and guys in the back of the truck. "Vamos, vamos!" I heard them yelling as they jumped out holding machine guns, then stood in a line facing my house. I realized there was another identical truck that had come from the other direction, from which five more guys ran to join the first group. A ten man firing squad. My mother's scream pierced the air, announcing a deafening roar of gunfire.

Suddenly, I was in the middle of a shootout. Bullets shattered the windows and tore through the walls, we were showered with blood and broken glass - Hell rained down upon us. I remember ducking behind the kitchen table as the dead bodies of my brothers and sisters fell around me, and I watched as my mother was struck twice, stumbled and fell. "Go!

Go!" she shouted, pointing at the back door through clouds of dust as the endless barrage of destruction continued for what seemed like an eternity. Terrified, I hesitated. I was only five years old, and I was forced into the position of having to leave my family to die. "Go now!" she screamed with all of her remaining strength. The last image I have of my mother is her burning the last of our family photos as she lay there dying.

Finally I ran. Out the back door, into the street, away from my family, away from my childhood, away from "John", the boy I was once and would never be again. The next thing I remember is banging on the door of a church, my clothes soaked in blood, screaming, "They're going to get me! They're going to get me!" The door opened and the face of an old nun appeared, and I felt relief wash over me. It may as well have been the face of God Himself. At that point, everything goes black.

CHAPTER 2

The next memories I have are of life in the orphanage. I believe now that the trauma of witnessing the slaughter of my family and the brutal conditions of the orphanage have obscured many of the memories I have of this time, as if my brain has shut me off and protected me from them. But I will do my best to share with you the little that I do remember, to give you an idea of where I truly come from, so that later in this book you can share in the joys of where life has taken me.

It was a life of total poverty. Countless children of all ages packed into filthy rooms and piled into stiff bunk beds stacked to the ceilings. We did not have clothes, only the gowns you might see on mental patients in old movies, and we did not have shoes. We were forced to walk barefoot on the dirty floors throughout the dilapidated facility. I remember tearing off a piece of the sleeve of my gown and tying it around me as a belt to better shield my back from exposure to the elements and the other kids.

We were at the mercy of the nuns that ran the orphanage, the only adults I remember from that time. Some were pleasant and kind; others were not. At lunchtime a bell would ring and we would file into the cafeteria and into a line with our wooden bowls. The nun that served us, the lunch lady, had a bad energy, one that I can still feel, and which seemed to transfer into the daily gruel she dumped in front of us without a smile. The food was not very good, usually thin soups with small amounts of rice or beans, and it often made me violently ill. There were many nights that I cried myself to sleep, from painful stomach aches, and the fear of what the next day might bring.

It was a violent life in the orphanage. Many of the other kids had come from similarly difficult backgrounds but hadn't taken it as well as I had. They were messed up. There was a courtyard of mostly dirt, with two rusty swings and a slide where we would be let out for outdoor time for several hours per day. At times it felt like a warzone. One instance of depravity sticks out in my mind, and should give you a good idea of what life was like there.

Pillows were a rare commodity. Most of us did not

have a pillow to sleep on at night, and everyone desperately wanted one, though I never did. As one of the younger kids living there, being given a pillow would have exposed me to unwanted attention from the older, more aggressive kids. When we received a few new pillows, probably from charitable donations, everyone would rush up to whichever nun handed them out and cry and beg to be chosen. One day, one of the boys in my room got one. As soon as the nun left, a fight broke out between him and an older kid, and I watched as strangled the younger boy to death. Over a pillow.

This was life as an orphan in South America in the 1980's. Most of us were used to violence. Kids came and went often - we were faceless and nameless. I'm sure that even the Sisters had difficulty distinguishing us. I don't think I ever made a friend there. In our gowns, floating through the darkened, crumbling halls, we were like ghosts in purgatory. I didn't think I would ever leave, I didn't even understand that leaving was a possibility or what it might mean. It was my harsh new reality, and for a year I survived. Alone.

Then came the day that an excited, bewildered commotion amongst the kids playing in the courtyard drew my eyes to two people walking with the nuns along the pathway towards the entrance to the building. Today, with the internet giving us immediate access to people around the world, it is difficult to imagine, but I had never seen Americans before. Their clothes, the way they carried themselves - they were like aliens. The children ran over to the fence to get a better look, shouting, calling out to them for attention, but I just watched. Then, for a moment, our eyes met, mine and those of the two mysterious strangers from another planet. They smiled, then disappeared inside and soon, the day continued as if nothing had ever happened. I'm sure that I myself came to forget about that moment.

The two aliens.

Some time passed. I'm not sure if it was days, weeks, or months, but I know that one afternoon, I was sitting in the courtyard and felt a bony hand on my shoulder, the hand of one of the older Sisters. This was personal contact that I was not used to there, and it struck me as odd. She took me into the building, through the halls and into a room I had never seen before. I was washed, cleaned up, groomed, given sneakers and clothing - it was like I was being presented for sale - and was then led into another strange room, where I was given strange toys: two little cars, one red and one yellow. I had never seen toys like this before and I was drawn to them instantly, falling to the floor, crouching, pushing them back and forth, crashing them into each other gleefully as all boys do, I didn't even realize I had been left alone - it was probably the first time in my life that I was in a room by myself. Soon, the door opened, and the two aliens appeared before me again. They were Drs. Charles and Ellen Prohaska. And I was going home with them.

CHAPTER 3

I didn't know it then, but a grueling 2 year journey had led them to me. It wasn't until I was 25 years old that I learned the reason my mother had gone to South America for adoption was because she wanted a child that had no chance of a good life otherwise. In me, she found what she was looking for. They had chosen me when we locked eyes that day in the courtyard. The following two weeks had been spent arranging all of the complicated legal aspects of adoption like U.S. citizenship, a passport, etc. and finally, on that day, they met their son for the first time.

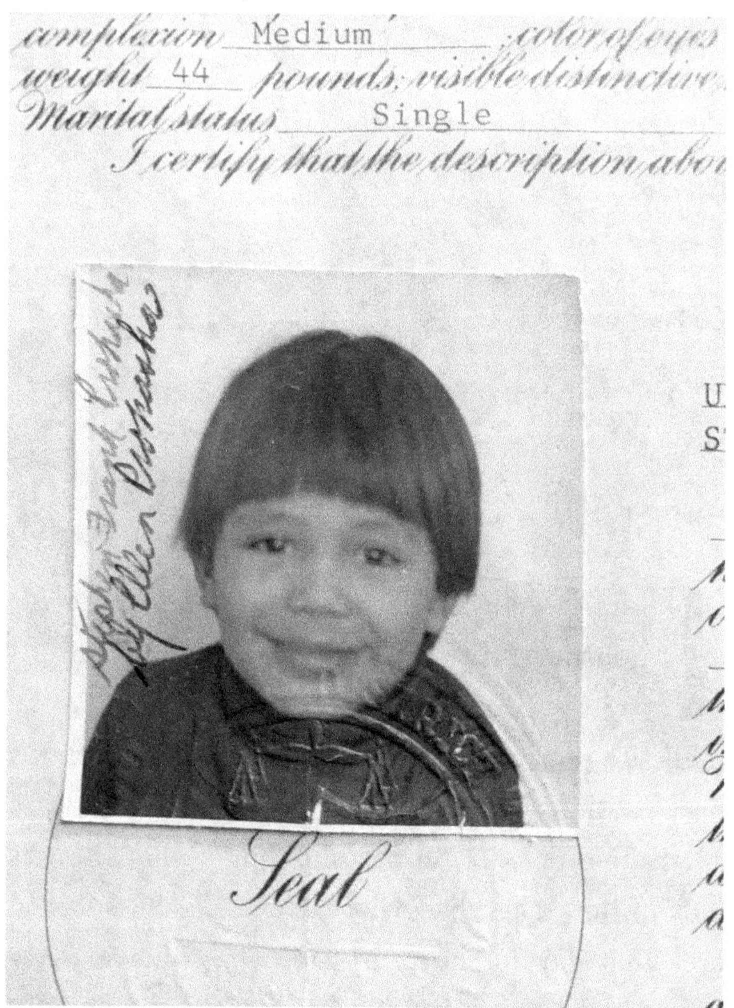

A photo taken at the orphanage agency, pasted onto my adoption paperwork.

He was an older man, about 60, wearing dockers and a collared shirt, with a clean cut beard and kind eyes that seemed magnified by thick, large-framed glasses. She was a bit younger, skinny, in jeans and a t-shirt, with long, dark curly hair, and she was more reserved and distant. Conversations between them and some of the Sisters followed, then my new father put a hand on my shoulder and led me away from the place I had called home for over a year.

Though my parents spoke decent Spanish, it was different, I guess a different dialect, and there were gaps in communication from the beginning. But even if they were perfectly fluent in the Colombian Spanish I was familiar with, I'm not sure I would have truly understood what was happening. At 6, it's diffi-cult to grasp adult concepts like adoption, and I don't remember being aware of it in the orphanage. At first, I'm sure that I was just relieved to get a break from the orphanage and happy to be getting attention from these nice-looking people that emanated class and money. I was even happier when we went straight to the barbershop and little Steve got his first haircut - we didn't get haircuts in the orphanage, and it was much needed.

Then we went to the hotel. The accommodations were much nicer than anything I had ever experi-enced, but I was confused and apprehensive. My father was very soothing, calm, always placing a soft hand on my shoulder at the right time, but my mother didn't know how to handle things. She was so excited to be a mother, and had been the propelling force through the adoption process, two years of difficult work that culminated in this moment, and I think it may have been too much for her. She just wasn't as engaged. This was the beginning of a lifelong trend - I would always be closer to my father. But the truth is, that night in the hotel, it didn't matter what they said or did. I was sleeping in a room with two strangers who were telling me that I was going to be living with them, going to America, to Connecticut, a place I had never even heard of before. I didn't believe or understand any of it, and I didn't have any time to. Things were moving fast.

The next day, we were at the airport. In Colombia, kidnappings are so common that even as a child I was aware of them, and in the noisy commotion of the airport, as airplanes took off in the distance, this is what I thought was happening to me. I ran, screaming, causing a major scene that attracted the attention of airport security. We were taken into the security office, where my parents were forced to produce the various documents that proved, legally, that I was their son. Soon, security escorted us onto the plane to ensure that there would be no further issues. I must have been calmed down well enough - the plane took off, carrying me away from my home country, away from my old family, and towards a confusing, frightening new beginning. It probably goes without saying, but this was my first time on an airplane.

Some hours later, we landed at JFK airport in New York City. I remember our walk through the terminal vividly. I was overstimulated and anxious, looking for opportunities to flee, while my parents took the opportunity to get closer to me in their own ways. My father tried to make it fun, asking if I wanted to go into each of the shiny stores that were entirely alien, yet exciting to me. My mother was one step removed, as if she were studying me, my body language, my reactions, what I liked and what I didn't like. By the time a child is 6 years old, as I was then, their parents know these things about them. In this case, they didn't have the slightest idea what might set me off and frighten me, or what might put a smile on my face and allow me to let my guard down. We passed a McDonald's and they asked if I'd like to eat there. I didn't even know what McDonald's was.

We exited the terminal and walked across the street to the parking lot, where their gray Datsun sedan was waiting for us. As we pulled out of the lot, I watched out the window as a plane took off in the distance. In my mind then, I identified it as the plane that had taken me to this strange place, and watching it disappear into the horizon struck fear into my heart, confirming something for me - there was no going back. Again, the feeling that I was being kidnapped overwhelmed me, and yet I was conflicted. My life in Colombia, in the orphanage, had been a nightmare, but such drastic, involuntary change in such a short time was scary. And if these two people were indeed my kidnappers, they were the nicest ones I had ever heard of. It was a fight within my own mind, a fight with myself and a fight with them, a fight that began in the Datsun and in some ways is still going to this day.

The car ride felt like an eternity. I had never traveled so far in my entire life, and the passing images of New York overwhelmed me, a feeling that continued even as the city faded behind us as we gradually drove deeper into the suburbs. Eventually, we arrived at my new home: a gray, 4-bedroom house in Trumbull, CT, an upper-middle class suburb about two hours from NYC.

The house in Trumbull.

To me, it was a palace, but it had not registered that this was now my home. I was excited, but confused as my parents took me into every room of the house, my father rubbing my back reassuringly as he encouraged me to open doors, look through cabinets, eat whatever I wanted, trying to communicate that this was all mine. "Why are you showing me this shit?" I thought, particularly bewildered as they opened the door to a pristine bathroom and attempted to explain that it was mine and mine alone. My bathroom? Mine? I didn't understand.

The living room.

By the time they took me to a bedroom, stuffed with toys and plush linens, comforters, cushions, pressed and cleaned, night had fallen, and it was time for bed. I was not used to having a bed of my own, certainly not one this nice, and it speaks to how uncomfortable and hesitant I was that I decided to sleep on the floor, on the right side of the bed. It wouldn't be until my third night there that I would finally feel comfortable enough to sleep in the bed. My parents took some pillows and a blanket and dropped them there for me, tucking me in as best they could, then they said goodnight. As they walked out of the room, they turned off the light and shut the door behind them, which triggered a deep fear inside me. I cried out and asked them to leave the light on and the door open, and they did, leaving me alone, another concept that was mostly foreign to me.

As I lay there on that first night, I thanked God that I didn't have to fight for the pillows and blankets that covered and cushioned me on the carpet, that at least for this night, they were mine. For a while, I was unable to sleep, my heart and mind racing, the anxiety and confusion of the situation still coursing through me. I was in a strange country, in a strange house, where two strangers had taken me to this strange room. I struggled to process it all, sweating and tossing and turning for hours from the sheer effort. Eventually, though, exhaustion began to creep over me and the anxious pounding of my heart and mind faded. I drifted into sleep, a sleep that was the best I had ever felt, and which lasted for what seemed like years.

CHAPTER 4

The next few weeks consisted of me getting used to my new life, one that was so radically different from the one that I had been accustomed to that at first it felt like an out of body experience. There is no how-to book on this process, and for my parents this was a time of consistent trial and error as they tried to learn everything they could about me and help me acclimate to the American way of life. They introduced me to new foods, hamburgers, spaghetti, barbecue chicken - I had never seen a hot dog before. At first I ate like an animal, with my hands, shoveling food into my face as quickly as possible, something I was forced to do at the orphanage due to the constant fear that it would be stolen by another child if it sat too long. I had to be taught that this food that was laid in front of me was mine, and no one was going to take it. Gradually, my father helped me learn how to use utensils.

It was this concept of "ownership" that was difficult for me to grasp. I had never owned anything before. My parents had filled the house with toys in anticipation of my arrival, and a consistent stream of them came through the front door, a result of my parents' well-intentioned efforts to give me as much attention as possible in that early period. GI Joes, action figures, electronic toys from Radio Shack that had buttons and switches and made titillating noises. They excited me of course, but it took time for me to understand their purpose, that they were there solely for my enjoyment, that I could play with them whenever I wanted and for however long, and if I put them down they would be waiting there for me whenever I might feel like picking them up again.

It may be difficult for some to understand, but there is an independence that children of a certain privilege have that was entirely foreign to me. A time came, after breakfast, when my parents were off doing their own thing, a time that was mine to do whatever I wanted with it, a big house with countless rooms to explore, filled with toys that I could bring into a large backyard where I could have imaginary adventures and play and have *fun* - but I had to learn how to have fun. This is the small, interior world of a child, yes, but to me it was a confusing one. In the orphanage I had always been told where to go and what to do, and in my home in Cali, I was too young to develop those instincts.

There was a closet full of clothes in my bedroom, but for those first couple of weeks I didn't open it. At the end of the day, I would drop my dirty clothes in a pile on the floor, and put them back on the next morning. I had to be painstakingly taught that those dirty clothes were to be put into a hamper where they would be washed at the end of the week, and each day a different set of clean clothes would be chosen, and the cycle would repeat. You might think this would be an easy thing to grasp, but it's a complicated matter of understanding. The closest thing I can compare it to is if you were trying to teach an animal human concepts. It's not as simple as pointing to the hamper and the closet - they might be able to do this once or twice, but they will not carry it with them forever unless they have an innate understanding of *why* they're doing it.

For the first few nights, I went to bed with my sneakers on, refusing to take them off out of the simple fear that they would be taken from me if I let them out of my sight, another result of what I had gone through at the orphanage. When I did become comfortable enough to take them off before bed, I made sure they were never too far, and left them at the foot of my bed, a ritual that continues to this day, and which even my kids have inherited. These were the beginnings of my introduction to American society, to the American way of life, and the progress had to come fast. When a child is adopted, certain things must be in place, including school registration, and there are legal timelines that must be followed. Only two weeks after I had arrived in the United States, I would be starting first grade.

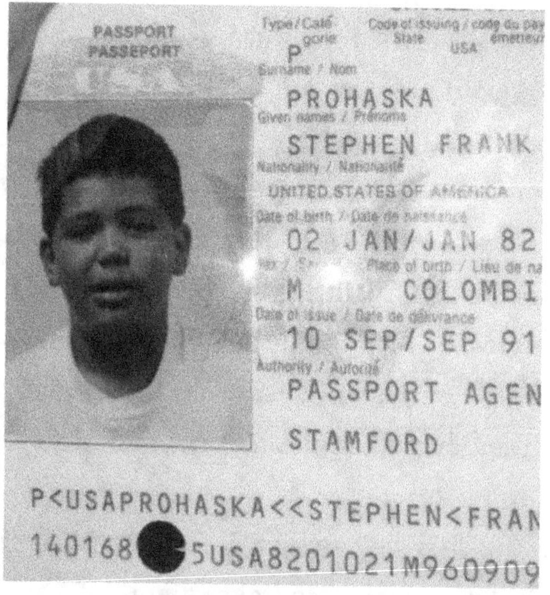

My American passport, a symbol of my transition into life in the United States.

Trumbull, Connecticut is a well-to-do suburb in

Fairfield County, which also contains wealthy towns such as Greenwich and Westport. According to the 2020 census, Trumbull has a population of 33,000, and is 72% White and 10% Latino. In 1986, when I arrived there, that Latino population seemed to consist of only one person - me. My parents seemed like aliens at first, and I had gotten somewhat used to it. But my school was an endless sea of aliens, in the halls, in my classroom, the students, the teachers, the administrators, the nurse, the lunch lady, the coaches. It has to be emphasized how much more isolated different cultures were from each other in that time. I hadn't even seen an American movie or TV show before I arrived in the country myself. It's not just the different skin tones and different languages. Those are obvious, and of course differentiated me from the others on an immediate surface level. In fact, because my parents had only spoken to me in Spanish since I had been adopted, I didn't even understand that everyone else only spoke English. But it's the clothes and the way the other kids wore them, the way they carried themselves, their body language, their attitudes, these small things you would never notice if you had been born here but made everyone feel so foreign to me then. I'm sure they felt the same about me.

Over the next several months, I slowly became

acclimated. My father was already retired when they adopted me after a long career as a mathematics professor, and he was the one that would cook our meals and take me to and from school, while my mother worked, herself a distinguished professor at Southern Connecticut University. Growing up I thought every father stayed home - I was lucky that mine did. We became very close, and if it weren't for his crucial, calming guidance in those early days I'm not sure what would have happened to me. I remember him and my mother teaching me English, in which I also got a crash course during school. There were no ESL classes then - everything was in English, and it was difficult at first, but it helped me learn faster than I would have otherwise, and though I started late, it would eventually become so ingrained in me that it now feels almost as if it were my first language. For a while, though, I would sit there in class, unable to understand the teacher, and look around me. The kids were all clean-cut and well-groomed, with nice clothes and nice things, colorful brand new bookbags covered in stickers of characters from TV shows and movies that I didn't know. It was so different from what I was used to.

From the moment I had arrived in the U.S., there had been constant change, a constant stream of information for me to process. I realize now that I had to understand this new life before I would be able to formulate any feelings about it. It took several months for me to become familiar with the rhythms of my new lifestyle, to become acclimated to it. Only then did I begin to see things that I didn't like. Rather than feeling more comfortable, the differences between myself and everyone around me seemed to have become exaggerated. My parents were white, my classmates were white, my teacher was white, the lunch lady was white. It had been some time since I had been around someone like me, and I was feeling it. When I walked into the classroom, everyone knew I was different, including me. For everyone else, there was an easy, seamless synchronicity and comfort as they moved through the day, from the classroom to the cafeteria to the playground outside. This only made me feel more isolated, feelings that carried over into my house. I didn't know how to deal with it.

The other kids began to make fun of me. These are the instincts of children when they encounter someone different, and I don't blame them, but it affected me deeply then. I badly wanted to become a part of their world, but it would be a few years before I truly would. My desire to fully acclimate only exacerbated my growing feelings of frustration. I often ate lunch alone, and even when I did eat with other kids, we simply couldn't understand each other. More frustration, more isolation - it was all too much.

Eventually, those feelings boiled over, and I began to act out. This started about six months after I was adopted, and it put a strain on our household. It was mild at first - talking back in school and at home, pouting, a nasty attitude, refusing to do anything and everything my parents asked of me. I remember snapping at my teacher in Spanish, and that my parents were brought in for meetings with her and the principal. My parents had a kind of good cop/bad cop dynamic. My father's way of showing love was tender and understanding - my mother was the disciplinarian. But in the beginning, she didn't know how to punish me when I acted out. All she knew about how to be a mother she had read in books. During the two year adoption process, she had felt only excitement and happiness. Now there were problems she hadn't anticipated, and there were no solutions in the books she had read. This was personal. Complicating everything was how new it all was. From the moment I had arrived, they had only thought of how to make me as comfortable and happy as possible. Now, only 6 months in, they were faced with the daunting prospect of having to discipline me. They knew they had to show me that what I was doing was wrong. But how far should they go? What if they crossed a line, what if they triggered something in me and scared me off permanently?

My mother was stern, and she challenged me. This would continue for the rest of her life, and I see now the positive impact it had on me, and the way it influenced my own personality - with my own kids, and in my life overall, I am confrontational, and I challenge others as she did me. But back then, her tough-love approach only made me feel more alone, and my behavior worsened. I started to steal, at first small things from the store like packs of gum and lighters, whatever I could fit into my pocket. My parents couldn't understand why I was doing this - I had everything I needed and more at home. But the stealing continued. One day, while she wasn't looking, I took a letter opener and jammed it into the ignition in my mother's car. Somehow, the car started, and I took it for a short-lived joyride down the block. I repeated this once more, this time with a stranger's car in the supermarket parking lot - at that point, my parents made sure not to leave letter openers lying around the house.

I developed an obsession with fire. I believe this was due to that lasting, final image of my birth mother burning the last of our possessions on the day she died. I started lighting fires everywhere, most often in our driveway, where I would pour gasoline or lighter fluid onto the pavement in an oily pool and toss a match or a Zippo lighter into the middle of it, finding some pleasure or comfort in the small explosion of flames. Later, my mother would jokingly refer to me as "little pyro" but at the time, my dangerous outbursts caused her a great deal of stress. Years later, I would find out that she had been so exasperated and disheartened by her failed efforts to reign in my terrible behavior that she considered giving me up. My father insisted that I only needed to be shown love and I would find my way. As usual, he was more in tune with my feelings and knew how to direct them towards something positive. He taught me how to build campfires as a way of speaking to that dark part of me that wanted to see things burn.

My mother continued to challenge me in her stern way as she tried to understand why I was acting out. I think both of their approaches were helpful, and I'm grateful for the balanced way they dealt with me. As for the reasons for my behavior, I know now that what I really wanted was attention and, ultimately, approval from my mother. Acting out was my way of trying to get that attention from her, as it often is in the mind of a child. In the coming years, I would slowly discover that there were positive things I could do to win her approval, and eventually I learned to channel my energy and aggression into schoolwork and sports.

But there were no signs of these positive developments then, and a time came when my parents knew more drastic changes needed to be made. About a year after I had first arrived, they agreed on a solution - little Steve would be getting a little brother.

CHAPTER 5

Over a year after I had been adopted, I found myself back at an orphanage in Colombia. For some reason, I don't remember if this was the same one that I had lived at, but I vividly remember standing with my parents, watching kids playing in a courtyard from behind a fence. It was as if we were shopping. I saw one little boy, a year or two younger than myself, and I don't know what it was, but something about him caused me to point and shout with excitement, "That's my brother!" That little boy was Mike, and indeed he became my brother on that day 35 years ago.

Me and Mike, gung-ho!

My parents had realized that one of the main
reasons for my difficult transition and poor behavior
was the absence of anyone that I could relate to. They
correctly identified my isolation at home and at

school as the source of many of the problems I was having, and decided to adopt another boy from Colombia as a way of helping me, and out of a desire to grow our family. As they often were, my parents were right. Mike and I were instantly close, and the happiness I felt when he came home with us was overwhelming. To have someone similar to me, someone to relate to, to communicate with, to share this new life with - it was a blessing. Mike had also become an orphan due to a traumatic family life - though his parents hadn't been killed, they had abused him, and we bonded over our difficult backgrounds. We also bonded over life in the strange new world of the United States. You can only imagine how much of a relief it was to be able to share all of this with him.

My parents, my brother Mike, and me.

The change was immediate and drastically positive. My brother's arrival marked a new stage of my transition, and I had become somewhat acclimated to my new life - finally, around 7, I was comfortable enough to begin to enjoy some parts of it and have fun. I started organized sports, which became an instant passion. I was a natural athlete, eventually winning awards in gymnastics and soccer, in addition to playing baseball. In sports, I found a place to take out some of those pent-up emotions that led to difficulties at home.

As my English improved I started to excel in school, garnering the approval from my mother that I had sought so desperately.

Life went on like this for a few years. At some point in that period, we moved to Southington, CT, another suburb about 30 minutes North of Trumbull. I started flag football, which also became a lifelong passion. But it was an unexpected part of that experience that left the most lasting impact on me. Like a lot of other kids in local organized sports, our team sold candy bars to friends and neighbors to pay for jerseys and equipment. But unlike most other kids, I took a different approach. Since I had arrived in the U.S., I had developed an obsession with making money. I think this was because I had so little in Colombia, and I started to understand how important money was, and how it represented the difference between life in the orphanage and my new, luxurious lifestyle in Connecticut. Selling candy bars provided me with my first real opportunity to apply this in real life, and I took full advantage. My teammates sold the candy bars for $1 apiece, as was instructed by our coaches and parents. I, on the other hand, realized that there was more money to be made.

The rich kids in school always seemed to have pockets stuffed with cash, and I saw their eyes light up at the box of chocolate bars that sat on my desk. I charged them $5 for each, and pocketed the differ-ence. This was the beginning of a hustle mindset that has turned me into the entrepreneur and busi-nessman I am today. Even then I was looking for any edge that could give me an advantage. One day, I returned home from school with an empty box of chocolate. My mother looked through my things, expecting the $140 I should have made. When she found $700 she was furious, and took it all. The lesson: never let anyone find out how much money you're making!

My brother and I continued to bond as we grew up together, and our family grew closer as Mike and I became more assimilated into the American lifestyle. By the time I was 10, both of us had transitioned fully into speaking fluent English, indistinguishable from the Native speakers that surrounded us. Now, we had really gotten into the groove, and the rhythms of life in Connecticut were natural to us.

My personality began to come out. I wasn't shy Steve or angry Steve anymore. I was funny Steve, the class clown that loved to make his family and friends laugh. I was becoming the extroverted Steve that I am today.

Little Steve, always making jokes.

There had been a steady stream of improvement for a few years, and overall in that time we were happy. But behind my desire to make people laugh, and hidden beneath my strong, outgoing personality, was a pain that I didn't fully understand. A pain that I kept bottled up in those years, but which grew steadily as I became more self-aware.

By the time I was 12 years old, I had been living in Connecticut for as long as I had lived in Colombia. I wasn't Esteban from Cali anymore - I was Steve Prohaska from Southington. Some of the more obvious things that had isolated me from the people around me in those first few years had subsided. There were no more barriers in language and communication, and the world that was so foreign to me at first had become my home. But as I got older and my mind developed, I became aware of the more subtle differences that a young child may not be able to grasp. I began to understand what it meant to be adopted, and just how different it made me compared to other kids. Again, I felt like an outsider, at school, and even more so at home.

Something that people don't understand about children of adoption is the nature of the relationship between them and their adopted parents. As much as they and everyone else tells you, the simple truth is they're not *really* your parents, and this is impossible to forget - at least, it was impossible for me. Now I compare it to what your relationship is with your best friend's parents, who's house you might have often slept over as a kid or teenager, who you may have gone on vacations with. They care about you, and do everything they can to make you comfortable, everything they can to make you feel at home with them. But inside you know that you're an outsider, and always will be. For me, this was the continuation of that internal battle that started the day I arrived here as we drove away from JFK airport, and around this time the pain that it caused me began to resurface.

My brother and I shared these feelings, and it was helpful to experience and understand all of it together, but we reacted differently to it. Mike was more introverted, and he kept to himself and occupied his time with hobbies like video games and collecting things. These were his outlets. Mine were sports and making people laugh, and for a while they were enough, but those feelings of isolation, that nagging feeling that I was an outsider, began to turn into anger directed at my parents.

It was that time, around 12 years old, that I started to rebel. Whatever my parents wanted, I wanted the opposite. If they were making chicken for dinner, I wanted steak. If they wanted me to go on a family outing, I wanted to stay home. If they wanted me to stay in, I was going out. I was always talking back, and I had a constant nasty attitude that often verged on meanness. I created a negative, contentious environment at home that was unsustainable. Something had to be done, for my benefit and theirs. By 13, I was going to 3 therapy sessions per week, two on my own, and one with my mother.

CHAPTER 6

My parents had identified the source of the problems I was having, but even with their balanced approach they were unable to get through to me. To them, therapy would be another outlet for me to talk through things that were happening inside my head, as well as an opportunity to communicate with each other in a new way, with the careful mediation of a professional to guide us. It is these family sessions, usually just between my mother and myself, that stick out in my memory the most, and they made me realize just how different our family was.

In front of the therapist, I felt empowered to speak openly about what I was going through, and how the things my mother did in response affected me negatively. I believe this helped her to better see things from my perspective, but it also raised in me a simple, but upsetting possibility: maybe I just didn't like her as a mother. Maybe she didn't know what she was doing. I had been brought into their lives from a difficult background. It shouldn't have been expected of me, I thought, to know how to handle it - I assumed they had all the answers, that their judgment was to be taken as fact. Now every-thing was blowing up. Why should any of the responsibility fall on me? "You came looking for me," I would say. "I didn't ask you to adopt me. You should've left me where I was." "We wanted to give you a better life," my mother would respond, to which I would reply, "It doesn't feel like a better life!" The argument would usually escalate from there.

In those early adolescent years, my bad attitude even extended to the therapists I was seeing. When you're a kid, the last thing you want to be told is that you should listen to your mother, and I didn't take it well. Every so often, I'd find myself in the office of a new therapist, going over the same problems. My father would accompany us at times, but him and I never really clashed. Was this because my mother had assumed the role of disciplinarian, or because he was always showing me love? If they both shared that more tender approach, would I have had those same problems? It was another internal debate that I was unequipped to deal with at that young age.

In a family therapy session, you are encouraged to speak your mind and say things you wouldn't during normal interactions at home. This is one of the reasons these visits can be helpful, and it allows more open and honest communication. But when your time is up, and inevitably your problems haven't been resolved, there is a lingering tension. Even today, thinking of my mother and I driving home from the therapist's office ignites anxiety in me. It was horrible. It felt to me then as if I had been snitching on a loved one, telling a stranger all the things about my mother that I didn't like. It felt wrong. As soon as the therapist set his yellow notepad down and pointed at the clock, the excitement and frustration of our arguments subsided and fear crept in. I didn't know how she was going to take the difficult things I said, things I never had and never would in any other circumstance. There was a painful awkwardness to those car rides - we couldn't just move on, talk about what we were going to have for dinner or what happened in school that day. Shit got too real, too personal.

My mother had a dominating personality, and so do I. Back then, this similarity caused us to clash in ways we didn't with my father or brother. Now, I see how this stern, domineering path she took in raising me informed my own pathway in life. She gave me thick skin, and she was always pushing and challenging me in school, in sports, in all things in life. I think to myself, at 41, "Damn. She made me strong." This was true love.

Despite the problems at home, life continued. Mike and I came further and further out of our shells as nature took its course. We had a group of close friends in the neighborhood - Ryan Scott, Audra, Erin and Ashley Grieves - and we would ride our bikes around together and play outside as kids did then.

Riding my bike around the neighborhood.

I remember that Audra was just a few houses down, and the Grieves sisters were a 5 minute ride away, and I had a crush on all three of them - though in Ashley and Erin's case, it may have had something to do with their go-kart. I developed a love for anything with wheels, and soon started to ride dirt bikes, the beginnings of another lifelong passion.

Riding one of my first dirt bikes.

As time passed, making people laugh became a signature part of my personality. That was who I was during childhood and adolescence, the clown, always looking to make someone smile. This is how I hid and treated the pain inside me, but it was true to my nature. Also true to my nature was the hustle mindset that emerged when I started scalping candy bars, and this continued to grow. I started stealing again, this time with a purpose. I would sell the stolen merchandise to classmates, whatever I could get my hands on. Zippo lighters were a hot commodity, and I remember grabbing them off the plastic case sitting on the gas station counter. My parents recognized these instincts in me and encouraged them.

It was during these years we began traveling the world. My parents would accept short teaching stints in foreign countries, and my brother and I usually tagged along. China, Germany, Peru - I learned about different people and became surrounded by other worlds. I'd see things in other countries I didn't see in America - different power outlets, butterfly knives, restaurants, currency. These lavish trips, amongst many other things, showed me that even amongst the upper-class people in our community, our family was particularly well-off. My parents were very, very successful, and it wasn't until around this time that I came to understand just how successful they were. I had developed a powerful obsession with dirtbikes, and only when I got older and started paying for it myself did I realize just how expensive an obsession it was, and how much my parents had spent to support it.

Despite my parents' wealth, and their position as highly intelligent, respected members of the commu-nity, and despite my outgoing personality, I started getting into trouble at school. I was in the 7th grade at

Depaolo Middle School at the time, and my parents began receiving phone calls from teachers and principals, who accused me of being present and responsible for various transgressions that took place on school property. The only problem - I wasn't present for any of the illicit acts I was accused of being involved in. Now, I realize that these were my first real experiences with legitimate racism. Kids joked when I was younger, sure, but that was just kids being kids. This had a serious impact on my ability to succeed in school, and I was beginning to get a bad reputation, one that was entirely unearned. I believe that because of my skin color and the way I carried myself, I was being blamed for things I had nothing to do with. Luckily, my parents agreed, and after one instance in which I was blamed for something that took place while I was actually with my parents, they decided to pull me out of Depaolo.

I was enrolled in St. Paul's, a private Catholic school in Bristol, Connecticut, before the beginning of 8th grade. My classmates were all rich white kids, and though we all wore the same uniform - shirt and tie, navy blazer, khaki pants - I stuck out because of the way I wore it, with my Jordan 6s on, and my clean haircut. I was the only minority in the school. The girls loved it - every day I was holding hands with a different girl. I don't even remember how many I made out with in the hallways there. In 9th grade I started lifting weights and getting some meat on my bones - the beginnings of Big Steve.

I wasn't long for St. Paul's - it was a very religious school, and I didn't consider myself religious at all. I remember one time, after breaking my leg in hockey practice, I made a joke during daily Church service - "God, please heal my leg!" The girls laughed, but the teachers didn't. They thought it was blasphemy.

CHAPTER 7

Before 10th grade, I was moved to Southington High, a much bigger school that fit me better than St. Paul's had. It was bigger in more ways than just the total number of students - I remember being struck with nerves as I stepped onto the field for football tryouts and got a glimpse of the sheer size of the guys I would be competing with. I had been lifting weights for over a year and was progressively getting stronger as I zeroed in on a favorite position - defensive end. If you watch football on Sundays, you know that the defensive end has to be the toughest, meanest motherfucker on the field to have any chance at getting to the quarterback. The offensive linemen at Southington High weren't as big as the guards, tackles and centers on your favorite NFL team, but they were a lot bigger than what I had been used to while playing in the private school division. Despite the nerves, I toughed it out and performed well enough to make the JV team. The excitement I felt when I saw my name on the roster wouldn't last - through my experience on the team, I would soon learn a harsh lesson about the adult world, one that was painful and frustrating at first, but ultimately served me well in the long run.

Going after the quarterback.

There was another kid on the team that played defensive end, Dave Robbins. Dave and I competed during tryouts, and he was one person that I wasn't nervous about. Everyone could tell that I was the better player, and I didn't even expect him to survive the final cut. When our head coach announced the starting lineups before our first game, I was shocked and disappointed to hear that Dave would be starting over me. I thought I had killed it at every practice and earned the starting spot. The teammates and coaches that I complained to agreed, and yet there I was, sitting on the bench. Dave was a weak spot on defense, and when I did get opportunities to play, I made a big impact. This was obvious to anyone watching, but week after week, it was more of the same.

I couldn't understand why this was happening. I worked hard, but nothing changed. I complained to my mother, "Why am I not starting? I'm better than these guys!". She didn't have the answers either. It wasn't until about halfway into the season that I learned that Dave's dad was a big booster for the school's athletic program. I soon came to understand that this was the reason that Dave was getting preferential treatment from the coaches, and why I was forced to sit on the bench for most of our games. It was a harsh realization - no matter how hard I tried, I was never going to start. There was an unspoken political element at play that I saw as an infuriating obstacle to my success at first, but I began to identify this confusing part of adult life not just in sports and in school but in our town and the way it was run. As I became aware of it, I learned to operate within it and use it to my advantage. This knowledge has been a vital part of my success as a businessman across every industry I've worked in.

I loved football, but by 11th grade, when I was on varsity, the infighting amongst the guys and that political element had me burnt out, and I gave up on it. But there were other things that occupied my time. At 15, I got my first real job, folding clothes at Filene's. I never wanted to ask my parents for money, and had a strong desire to support myself. I was interested in business, investing, entrepreneurship, and my parents encouraged this. Now that I was making money in legitimate ways, my mother made a deal with me. She would match anything I wanted to invest and help me buy stocks with it. If I gave her $500, she would put in another $500. I remember she bought me shares in Mcdonald's and Coca Cola amongst other companies. It would always put a smile on my face when I would see a Mcdonald's or a bottle of Coke in any of the foreign countries we visited, when I realized how international and iconic these brands were and that I owned a small part of them.

My parents were my primary role models at that time in my life, and they were the people I compared myself to. My father had graduated second in his class at Annapolis, and my mother first in hers at Purdue, and they both went on to distinguished academic careers after securing doctorates. Even amongst the wealthy, successful people in our upper-class community, my parents were extremely educated and intelligent. I believed then that this type of education was what I needed to strive for to be truly successful, and to be the best version of myself I could be. I also badly wanted to impress them and gain their approval, and in high school I thought the best way to do this was by getting good grades in school. I worked as hard as I possibly could, paying attention in class, doing my homework on time, and anything and everything I could do to be #1 at everything I did academically.

With my dad, before a family wedding.

Me and mom.

At 16 I got my license, and my parents bought me a van that I would use to explore the thing that had become my true passion - racing dirtbikes. I would load the van up with whatever bike I was riding at the time and all my equipment and head out. Every weekend I was on the racing circuit, traveling throughout New England to the best spots with the best competition - Jolly Rogers in New Hampshire, Marlboro, Massachusetts, Southwick, Central Village. I was obsessed.

That Summer I became a lifeguard at the public pool, working under Tony Palmeri who ran Southington Parks and Rec at the time. I gave swimming lessons and became head lifeguard the following Summer.

Me and the other lifeguards at the Southington public pool.

I put more time into my body and got myself into amazing shape. My mother enrolled me in business classes that further inflamed my love for all things money. I stopped going to therapy as things cooled off at home and our family became closer.

I had friends in school, through dirt bike racing and sports, but I wasn't into partying. I didn't drink much, and coming from Colombia I knew the truth about how bad drugs can be, and stayed away from those parts of teenage life. For the most part, I kept to myself. I would go to school and work, go to the gym, then put my dirt bike into the van and take off as soon as I got the chance. This was my life throughout high school.

Receiving my high school diploma.

CHAPTER 8

Because of my successful academic career and my interest in business, it was predetermined that I would be going to college before I even graduated high school. Coming from the world of academia themselves, my parents encouraged this and pushed me towards college, and I accepted this as inevitable. I didn't even know then that there were different paths that I could take. I graduated from Southington High School in June of 2000, and that Fall I moved into a dorm on the Southern Connecticut State University campus in New Haven, where I would major in business. Finally, Big Steve was on his own.

I fell in love with freedom instantly. I no longer felt the pressure to please my parents through academics, and became drawn to other parts of life that would define me as a man of my own. I made two best friends, and the three of us would party together what seemed like every night - I more than made up for those years in high school that I stayed away from alcohol and drugs. I don't think there was a single Saturday in those first two years of college that I woke up before 3 in the afternoon. I played intramural sports, and won multiple championships in foosball. I was doing a lot of casual dating, just having fun, without a care in the world. I was living it up, and finding myself while having the time of my life.

I didn't realize it then, but it wasn't all good. Thinking back, I'm not sure if it was the right time for me to go to college. My mother even said, years later, that if she could do it again she would have had me wait. When I got to Southern, the pressure of needing my parents' approval through academic success had faded. My work in school suffered - I just didn't care as much about classes as I did in high school. I had moved past the stage of my life when I was defining myself solely by my grades. There were more exciting parts of life to explore, more exciting things to become than a good student, and I became convinced early on that I didn't need college to be successful. I thought I knew everything I needed about business to go out on my own. It wasn't until later, when I had experience in the real world, that I realized how important college is for future success. When I worked $13 per hour jobs, and I saw that only the guys with college degrees get promoted and move up the ladder, I wished I had taken college more seriously from the jump.

The freedom of breaking out from underneath my parents' roof also proved to be too much for me to handle. I was eating like shit, always ordering out with the guys, and I put on the Freshman 15 and then some. The partying was fun, and it was necessary for me to find myself in the world, but I didn't know how to find the proper balance. I didn't even know that I had to. I wasn't taking care of myself. I needed to learn the discipline that truly separates the men from the boys, but it would be a couple years into my time at Southern before I would do so.

I did want to excel at what I was good at - business - but was usually too bored in class to care. In the rare times something in one of my business classes challenged and intrigued me enough, I gave 100% effort. One example from my Sophomore year stands out in my mind. One of my professors assigned us a project - we had to come up with a product of our own invention, one that could realistically be produced at that time. But there was a twist that got my attention - the project was really a competition to see who could come up with the best product. The professor would help the winner actually develop a business plan for their product and sell it to someone in the relevant field. I was fired up. I cooked up something that I still believe is a genius idea - pizza sticks. A slice of pizza, wrapped around a stick and frozen, to be bought in packs of 8 from your supermarket. You can have your pizza, without greasy hands. Pizza on the go.

Needless to say, I won the competition, and started working hard on my proposal. As luck would have it, my professor happened to be friends with the CEO of Frito Lay, and he arranged for me to meet with him about Pizza Sticks. They were going to put Pizza Sticks in supermarkets around the country. I saw dollar signs. But there was one problem - I had been assigned a partner in class. He had no part in developing Pizza Sticks, but legally he had to be considered a partner in the business. When his parents heard about our meetings, they got involved, and they blew the whole thing up over percentages. I was 19 years old, already thinking about how I was going to spend the millions I was going to make, and then just like that, it was over. That's life.

Most of the time during those first two years at Southern I spent learning about myself, slowly becoming the man I am today. I didn't talk to my parents often, and only went home for holidays and over the Summer. I was more interested in being free from them after all those years of living under their roof, and it was important that I had that time to discover who I was as a person out in the world on my own. In the Summers, I worked as a ride operator at Lake Compounce, an amusement park in Connecticut. I got a taste of what a regular job was like, and I saw the older guys that didn't go to college, who had the same job I did as a 19 and 20 year old. It made an impression on me - I didn't want to end up like that - and by the beginning of my Junior year at Southern, I decided that things needed to change.

In those first couple of years, I started to see glimpses of the real world, and something solidified that last Summer at Lake Compounce - my parents were right. College and education were important to my future success. I knew I had to make the most of my remaining time at Southern if I had any hopes of becoming who I wanted to be when I graduated. This realization only became more clear when, that Junior year, I started thinking about what jobs I might be able to get out of college. I wanted a managerial position, and I'd need to work hard to make that happen for myself, and finally, I was ready to give 100% effort in all aspects of my life. The discipline that I sorely lacked at 18 and 19 was beginning to become ingrained in my mindset, and I learned to become structured on my own. Structure is vitally important to continued success. When you're a teenager, you take life as it comes to you. Party until the sun rises, wake up whenever you feel like it, squeeze homework in if you can, miss class if you're hungover, skip the gym if you're tired. But successful adults don't live like that. Millionaires and billionaires have every second of their life scheduled.

This was the part of me that emerged Junior year. I excelled in all of my classes, learning the intricacies of business. I got into the best shape of my life, and even got a six pack.

Back to the grind.

My brother and I had grown apart once I got to

college, but he started to look up to me again. My parents were happy, and I was happy. Everything was finally coming together. In 2004, I graduated from Southern with a degree in business management, ready to take on the real world in my own way.

CHAPTER 9

Right out of college, I got a job as an assistant manager at Sherwin Williams in Brookfield and moved into my own one-bedroom apartment in Bethel, an apartment I would live in for a few years. I was selling paint, and I excelled at it immediately. I was a natural salesman, and I hit every quota I needed to and often exceeded them. But an ugly side of corporate life began to reveal itself to me. I was working my ass off, making the manager and the company a lot of money, but I never saw any of it myself. What the fuck? Why am I doing this shit, going the extra mile, if I'm not going to benefit from it? This is something they don't teach you about in business classes. It pissed me off, and I became disillusioned with the corporate world. I was willing to work hard if I had something to show for it, and taking a few cans of paint off the shelf didn't do it for me.

During that time, my friends and I liked to go out to different clubs in the area. One night, we were at one of my favorite spots, Tuxedo Junction in Danbury. I was having a good time and had a few drinks in me when these two guys started talking shit - I tried to walk away, but they just kept going, and at that point I had no choice but to knock those motherfuckers out, which I did easily. They don't call me Big Steve for nothing. After the altercation, I apologized to the bouncers for causing trouble, and me and my boys were on our way out the door when I felt a hand on my shoulder. It was the owner, Mike - I thought he was going to yell at me or call the police. Instead, he offered me a job. He saw how easily I had handled the two shit-talkers and asked if I'd like to work for him as a bouncer, just Friday nights to start. I said yes, and though I didn't know it then, it was the start of something that would in many ways define my life for the next several years.

Tuxedo Junction was a concert venue and club with a capacity of about 600 people. A lot of big names played there over the years, but even when there wasn't a name, the club was packed wall-to-wall with local college kids looking for a good time. This was heavy duty shit - an entire security team was needed on weekend nights. I would become close with a lot of the guys in my time working there, but from that first night I could tell I was different. The other guys on the team clocked in, did what they needed to do and clocked out, like it was just another job. But I fucking loved it, from the minute I took my place by the door on that Thursday night. The pretty girls kissing me on the cheek, the drinks flowing, the music, the cocaine - I knew then that this was the lifestyle for me. Hundreds of people were lined up outside waiting to get in, hoping that I would give them the nod. I was the guy holding the velvet rope. I was in charge. And it was intoxicating.

The owner, Mike Roviello, was an old-school Italian guy that was always in the back office making sure everything ran smoothly. He had decades of experience owning clubs and restaurants, and I could tell he knew his shit. I made sure to get close to him early on, as soon as I started to consider a career in nightlife. I was always asking Mike questions - how do you choose who to hire? How do you place orders? How do you count the money? Do you carry a gun? This also differentiated me from the other people working there. I couldn't believe that they weren't taking advantage of the wealth of knowledge available to them. I stayed in Mike's office hours after last call, trying to glean every valuable tidbit of information I could. He recognized how hard I worked and we became close, but inevitably he would get sick of me and shout, "Get the fuck out of my office!" I couldn't help it - I saw how much money these owners made, their lifestyles, tens of thousands of dollars every day and having fun while doing it. I wanted what Mike had. I had to start at the bottom, but the bottom wasn't so bad.

I was good at it, too - soon after starting with just Thursdays, I was put on Saturdays, then Sundays, then Fridays, and I became a fixture there all weekend long. Eventually, I was making more money bouncing than I was working full-time as a manager at Sherwin Williams. I considered quitting my job at the paint store, but the decision was made for me not long after I started at Tuxedo. One night, me and some friends were leaving Hooters, and we had all had a few too many. My boy was driving when he shouldn't have been, and he was swerving all over the road. I told him to pull over and let me drive. A few minutes later, I saw red and blue lights flashing in the rearview mirror. I was hit with a DWI, and my license was suspended. With my parents' help, I hired an attorney that was working to expunge the charge from my record and get my license reinstated, but in the meantime I had driven the Sherwin Williams van. My manager found out, and I was fired for driving a company vehicle without a license. I didn't mind - I was having too much fun.

Working the door at Tuxedo.

Even though I was having a blast, working security at Tuxedo was serious shit. We would regularly squeeze 900 people into the club, despite a legal capacity of 600. When there was any kind of trouble, I'd find myself taking on twenty or thirty guys at a time. We knew if there was a scuffle, we might not be going home - I always had on a stab vest, and even that wouldn't protect me from being trampled. I broke bones, broke guys jaws - it got to a point that my mother feared retaliation. The crowd would change depending on what music we were playing, and each had its own challenges. Thursdays were Thirsty Thursdays and that brought out a lot of the preppy white collar college kids. Fridays were Latin nights, Saturdays was rap and hip-hop. I never knew what the night would bring - it was exhilarating. As I got more and more involved in the operations of the club, I helped turn the team into a well-oiled machine, and we always had each others' backs.

I was fucking chicks, taking shots, blasting lines and beating guys up, all while learning the business. It was heaven, and I was excited to go into work every single night. How many people can say that about their jobs? Some time after being fired from Sherwin Williams, I knew I needed to take on another gig - this was the hustle mindset. Through the club, I met a guy named David that wanted to start a landscaping busi-ness with me. We bought some equipment, and David and I mowed lawns and trimmed hedges during the day, and on weekends I bounced at the club. I was making good money, but I wanted more, I wanted some fast, easy cash. David was pretty heavy into drugs, and through him I started selling a little cocaine on the side.

My boys and I were common fixtures at the various strip clubs dotting central Connecticut. I loved women, and had a different girl every week, sometimes multiple women in a week. There was a seemingly endless supply, a whole line of them every weekend at Tuxedo, and it wasn't exactly difficult for me whenever we went somewhere else. I was in the best shape of my life, I was making good money, I was always making people laugh - I was the life of the party. One night, we were at Alon strip club in Danbury, and a girl caught my eye, a girl I had never seen before. I can see her so vividly, dancing there on the stage that night. She was smoking hot, a 10 out of 10, unbelievable body, angel face, porcelain skin shimmering in the flashing lights. The truth is, she caught the eye of everybody in the club - it was as if time had frozen when she came out of the dressing room - but I was the only one that caught hers. She passed me as she walked off the stage - I motioned for her to come close and she leaned over as I whispered, "I'll pick you up out back."

I said goodbye to the guys, walked out to the brand

new BMW 740i I had recently bought and swung it around to the rear parking lot. I must have been quite a sight, sitting there in the idling car as she walked out of the club in street clothes. She got in and we wasted no time driving to the hotel she was staying at, and we fucked that night, and the following morning I left. Her name was Amanda, she was from Albania, and though she was memorable and sexy she was just one of a series of girls that I was seeing. In the following weeks I probably saw her a few more times in some similar fashion, the same routine, I don't really remember. But I do remember receiving a phone call a month or two after that first encounter when she told me that she was pregnant.

CHAPTER 10

I didn't believe it at first - she was a stripper, who knows how many guys she was fucking? We talked, and I became convinced that it was true, that she was pregnant and I was the father. It was agreed that we would have the baby, and Amanda moved into my apartment in Bethel. It all hit me like a truck. I was 25 years old, working as a bouncer and mowing lawns, and I had gotten a stripper pregnant. It was like I had become some depressing statistic. I was raised by two doctors, respected members of the community, who had given me a stable home and everything I had wanted. They had raised me right, and this is what I had become. I felt like life as I had come to know it and love it was over, and that I had let my family down.

I fell into a deep depression and began drinking

heavily. My work suffered - about two years into working at the club, Mike fired me - I was fucking around too much on the job, and he had had enough. Before I left his office, I promised him that I would come back and take his job one day - but that day wouldn't come for a while. David's problems with drinking and drugs had become too much to handle, and I terminated our business partnership and sold off my corporate landscaping accounts. Soon after, I got a job selling furniture at Raymour and Flanagan, but that didn't last long either. I thought that as a natural salesman it would be a good fit, but it made me feel dirty to push products on people that they didn't want just to get a commission. I realized it wasn't for me, and quit not long after Amanda and I moved in together. At that point, it was just me and her in the apartment with nothing to do but spend time together. As I began to learn more about her, things between us only got worse.

Amanda had been shipped to the United States at 19 as part of an arranged marriage with a wealthy contractor with ties to the Albanian mob. They had two daughters together, but her husband was violently abusive, and a few years after they married Amanda decided to run away. She got an apartment near their house in Mahopac, NY, and started dancing at clubs in Connecticut so that she wouldn't be known as a stripper locally. She would put herself up in hotels and hit different clubs to support herself, on her own in a strange country. That's what she was doing when she and I met. I soon came to understand how deeply troubled she was. She had come from an impoverished part of Albania and had received little to no education. She couldn't read or write, and had no practical knowledge of adult life. She also had severe mental health problems that I'm sure were due to her difficult life. She was crazy, and our relationship was dangerously toxic from the moment she moved in.

We tried to make it work. Through my nightlife connections, I was able to get her shifts stripping at the best clubs in the area on the nights she would make the most money. Every week we would do the circuit all over New England - Mardi Gras in Springfield, Kisses in Stamford, Alon in Danbury. When she became too pregnant to dance, my mother paid for her to get bartending training. My uncle Ira, a former immigration agent, helped her secure the green card she lost when her relationship with the father of her children blew up. I moved us into a bigger, nicer apartment in the Avalon, a luxury complex in Danbury, in advance of our child being born and so that we would have a little more room to breathe. But any attempt at helping her was just another fight between us. She had no interest in bettering herself or planning for the future. And motherhood? Forget it - I had no hope that she would be able to step up. I thought she was a loser, and felt like one myself by association.

My depression worsened. I was drinking a bottle of Jack Daniel's every day, and I had stopped working out, stopped taking care of myself. I was a mess. I couldn't avoid the constant feeling that I had let everyone down - my parents, myself, and my unborn child. Even with all the promise that I had, all the opportunity, the privileged upbringing I had been blessed with, after everything I had been through - this is what I had amounted to. Unemployed, with a 21 year old stripper that can't read as a baby momma. What kind of life would I be able to provide, especially with her as my partner? How can I win when I'm with someone that doesn't want to win herself? I was excited to have a child, but by the time I reached the weeks leading up to the due date, I had become numb to it all. That excitement, hidden beneath a hazy numbness, is what I remember feeling on August 14th, 2006 when Amanda's water broke.

I remember that my parents were there that day at Danbury hospital, and that I was fat as fuck, a result of my month's long depression. And I remember being totally numb, as if I were having an out of body experience, or watching a TV show about someone else's sad ass life. Yes I was excited to be a father, but I didn't know what to do, how I could possibly turn the situation around. I thought I was looking at a lifetime of struggle and toxicity that would hang over my child and myself like an endless, darkened cloud. Then a crown, and a push, then another, and then - there he was. My first child, in the flesh, glowing as the shafts of sunlight streamed in through the windows and caught the shiny wet patches that covered his little pink body. When I held him for the first time, everything changed. The numbness lifted and revealed an ultimate clarity. I had been raised in a traditional family, and I believed strongly that this was the best environment for my newborn son to grow up. I was determined to make it work with Amanda, to help get her life on track, to get my own shit together and bring us together as a family. For him. For Julian Charles Frederick Prohaska

We decided on Julian, a name that is represented in my Latin culture as well as Amanda's Albanian culture, as a show of appreciation and respect to our backgrounds. Frederick was the name of my mother's father, and Charles, of course, after my own father, a small symbol of the close bond we had developed over the years. And there was another person that I wanted to honor, to make an eternal part of my family by including him in Julian's name. Luckily, it was an easy and convenient fit.

When I walked onto the field for my first flag football practice at 9 years old, the sea of rich white kids parted and I saw a black boy standing there. His name was also Charles, like my father, and we became instant friends, drawn to each other as the only minorities on the team. We bonded over our shared differences as well as the unique struggles we faced in our own lives. I felt out of place in my own family, and Charles, coming from the projects, had lived a life of poverty. We felt at home with each other, and went through everything together - through all the schools, college, jobs, the ups, the birth of my son, Charles was there. I hoped he would be like another uncle to him, and for a while, he was.

One night, about two years after Julian was born, my cell phone died and I didn't think anything of it - I tossed it on my bedside table and went to sleep. Charles was working in Rhode Island at the time, and had taken a girl out on a date. He was walking her home when a man rushed towards them holding a pistol - Charles shielded the girl from harm as the man opened fire on them and bullets pierced his flesh. The gunman jumped into a waiting car and drove off, and Charles' date fled in fear. Charles was able to crawl inside his apartment and call for help, and was taken to the hospital where he was soon joined by his sister. With Charles in critical condition, his sister tried to call me - but the call went straight to voicemail. My phone was dead. By the time morning came and I heard the devastating news, Charles had passed. I lost the opportunity to say goodbye to my best friend. From that day forward, I have always made sure that my phone is fully charged, no matter what.

The police never found Charles' killer. My understanding was they believed his date was the one who had been targeted, but I guess that was a dead end. My father loved Charles, and as a highly intelligent man that was deeply puzzled by the tragedy, he looked into the circumstances himself and developed his own theory. Charles worked for a cleaning company that was owned by a wealthy man that was suspected of being involved with the Mafia - let's call him Mike. A few days before his death, Charles had applied for a license to start a cleaning company of his own. My father believed that this business was a front, the first part of Mike's plan to establish a monopoly on cleaning services in the area and hike rates, and that Charles murder was a hit ordered by rival mobsters as a warning aimed at Mike. Whatever the circumstances surrounding his death may have been, I'm glad that Charles' memory lives on in the hearts of many - myself, his nieces and nephews, the rest of his family - and in the name of my son.

Charles and I, having a good time as we always did.

CHAPTER 11

Julian Frederick Charles Prohaska. That was his name, and I was determined to give him the world, starting with a loving, stable home environment. We took him back to the apartment in Danbury, and my immediate mindset was that I needed to make it work with Amanda. I tried, tried as hard as I had at anything in my life, but it became clear almost immediately that rather than bring us closer together, Julian's birth had drawn Amanda and I further apart. The toxicity and fighting had only intensified. I was trying to plan our future, but she only hindered these efforts. I felt like I was carrying dead weight, if dead weight fought with you every possible second. Her own life seemed to be falling apart as she continued to spiral. She had no family in the country, no friends - she was even forbidden from seeing her two daughters because she had a child with someone outside of her own Albanian ethnicity. I only saw them twice in the entire time we were together, and to this day Julian has never met his half sisters. I felt for her, but she was resistant or perhaps just apathetic towards any kind of legitimate help or change. The resentment I felt towards her was approaching a breaking point.

That breaking point came one night about two months after Julian was born. We were fighting, as we always seemed to be, and she kept repeating a line that had become her signature - "You don't care about me!" In the past, I had deflected, ignored it, or in my better moments assured her that it wasn't true. But this time was different. I had had enough. This time I let it all out. I told her that she was right - I didn't really love her. I was trying to do the right thing, trying to be a good man and father, trying to turn us into a family. I told her that I was only with her because we had a son together. This hurt her deeply, and my brutal honesty vaulted her past a breaking point of her own. She snapped. She said if I didn't love her, then she was going to destroy the one thing I did love.

Before I was able to react, she grabbed Julian, a two month old infant, and ran out of the apartment and onto the busy street. She was trying to get hit by a car, to kill herself and our child. Cars veered, horns blared, headlights illuminated her crazed, widened eyes. I sprinted after her, grabbed Julian out of her arms, and dragged her back onto the curb, both of them crying, my heart pounding, a chaotic and dangerous situation that could have been worse. Two things became clear to me in that moment - that Amanda was completely fucking psycho and could never be a mother, and that I needed to do something drastic in my own life to make up for my child losing a parent. That I needed to get back on track. I put Julian in my car, and drove to the one place I knew we would be safe, where I could put the pieces of my life together. My parents' house.

It was decided that I would have sole custody of Julian, and for the foreseeable future we would be living with my mother and father. Amanda didn't put up a fight, and I paid the rent on our apartment for the remainder of the lease so she wouldn't be out on the street. I was relieved, and happy to be free, but my parents were even happier. They had adopted my brother and I when we were already 5 years old, and this was the first time they would have a baby in the house. They were more than willing to take on a share of the responsibility in raising Julian, and I was blessed to have them. They were wonderful parents to me, and I knew they would be wonderful grandparents. With their help, and with the weight of my toxic relationship with Amanda now lifted off my back, I was free to rediscover myself as a man. After getting settled, I turned to the industry that had most captivated me - nightlife.

Through connections I made in my days at Tuxedo Junction, I was able to get a job managing two strip clubs in Waterbury, CT, Peekaboo and Happy's. I was a natural fit and was excited to be back in the game. All of those hours I spent as a bouncer and in Mike Roviello's office learning the operational side of a nightclub proved to be invaluable as I stepped into my first managerial role in the business. I was in charge of staffing, ordering food and drinks, security - all the day-to-day operations - and had to make sure it all ran smoothly. Much of this was already familiar to me after the time I had put in working under Mike, and I hit the ground running, but I soon realized that the differences between running a strip club and a regular nightclub were more stark than I had expected.

Managing staff at a strip club is a totally different game. At any other kind of bar or restaurant, you hire whoever you think will do the best job, and there are a lot of different kinds of people to choose from. But strippers have to have a certain look, and there are a lot of girls with that look that won't even consider stripping. It's much harder to find the right dancer than the right waiter or bartender at a regular club. You end up having to manage personalities, a difficult proposition when it comes to hot girls in their early twenties. They were talent, like you might have on a movie set. They expected to be treated like stars, and some of them had movie star attitudes.

Scheduling was like deciphering a puzzle - which girl has to watch her kid because the father went to jail, which girl just got taken on a trip to Jamaica by a customer from last week - every night it was something new. It was a nightmare to put it all together - with one club, it would have been difficult, with two it was almost impossible. I fired a lot of girls - we had plenty of turnover - but in a lot of ways, I was at their mercy. And these were hood chicks, tough as nails, and they didn't like to take shit or be told what to do.

The clubs were in a rough part of town, and they attracted a rough crowd. I came to understand why the owners always had guns on them. When I started, shootouts outside the clubs and fights inside were as common as lapdances. Our customers were street kids, gangsters, drug dealers. I knew I had to set a different tone. I tried implementing a lot of the methods that I had success with as a bouncer at Tuxedo, and I made an impact, but the security guys at Peekaboo and Happy's didn't have the passion and energy that I had when I was in their position. They just wanted to go home at the end of the night. Truth be told, I couldn't blame them. There was a darkness to the strip club industry that was slowly revealing itself to me.

The owners insisted on rules and regulations that would keep everything legal, and for the most part I abided by them. But I learned early on that there are certain things you have to let slide to keep both customers and dancers happy. When the owners weren't around, the girls would throw me a couple bucks on their way to a backroom with some dude with a hard-on. I knew what was going down based on the "commission" they gave me so that I'd look the other way. $5 meant a $25 handjob, $10 meant $50 blowjobs, $20 meant the $100 full package. It was nasty, dirty shit. But that was the business.

I started selling coke again, this time to customers at the clubs, and it was a great secondary source of income. I started using pretty heavy, a way to stay alert on those late nights. With that crowd, I needed it. Once I got settled and into a routine, things were running pretty smooth. I had reestablished a life for myself, rediscovered myself as a man, and I felt great. Julian was healthy and happy in the stability and comfort of my parents' house. He took his first steps, said his first words. My mother and father were loving every second of it. They had fully embraced their role as grandparents, and I'm not sure what I would have done in that time without their help. Just as I had as a child, Julian developed a particularly special relationship with my father - he loved that kid so much, it makes me emotional now, thinking about them together during that time. I had improved business at the clubs, I was selling coke, making good money, and life back home proved to be just what I needed. Life went on like this for a couple years, and it was good. But I wanted better for myself. I wanted more.

CHAPTER 12

Even though I was doing well for a guy in his late 20s, with a healthy son and a decent-paying job, I couldn't shake the feeling, deep down, that I was a failure. I wasn't married, and my baby momma was an absentee stripper. I didn't have a doctorate, I wasn't a respected member of the community, I wasn't an esteemed professor - I was working at strip clubs and selling drugs. To me, coming from the environment that I was raised in by my parents, that made me a loser. But they saw past that, even if I couldn't. They watched as I grew into my managerial position and became more educated in the world of nightlife. They listened to my stories about the dirtbag owners and how I was working my ass off for them. They recognized that I had identified an industry that I was passionate about and excelling in. About a year after I started at Peekaboo and Happy's, they decided that I was finally ready to realize my true potential.

I can see it so clearly, and hear the words as if he's speaking them to me now. My father sat me down one night, and said "Steve - you're going to run your own business." I couldn't believe it, I didn't understand. Me? A business of my own? What kind? He asked what I liked to do most on my nights off, how I liked to spend my free time. I told him I liked to go out - like any young guy might, but I more than most. I absolutely loved it. The atmosphere, the excitement, the danger, the women, the drugs, the money - it was everything I ever wanted. And he told me that if that was the case, then I was going to run my own club. I said, "What do you mean? I'm already doing that." "No," he said, "you're going to own one." By then, he was 80 years old, and knew he didn't have much time left. He wanted to give me one final gift, after all the priceless ones he had given me in all those years, and help me see it to fruition before his time was up. He said that if I could find the right spot, he would help me pay for it. Big Steve was getting a place of his own.

I was ecstatic, and eternally grateful for the opportunity. Our relationship was always so special, and the fact that he trusted and believed in me in that incredible way only strengthened it. I was going to do it right, and I got started immediately. Every day I looked at each of the commercial brokerage sites, pouring over every listing. My parents and I would check out the places with good specs, but couldn't find the right fit. This went on for about a year, but I kept at it.

One day, I was looking at a listing on auto-pilot - I had looked at so many and it had become such a routine, I had become somewhat numb to it. Capacity, 600...live music...open 25 years...Danbury...this seemed familiar. Wait a second - I know this place! I used to work there! It was my first love - Tuxedo Junction - and it was for sale. I saw a dream coming true before my eyes, and though I didn't love my chances, I knew I had to do everything I could to make it a reality. Worried about the bridges I had burned there, I made an appointment to view it without using my real name. When I arrived, Mike's co-owner Al Cacomo, who had been less present in day-to-day operations of the club when I worked there, greeted me. He didn't recognize me at first, and introduced himself, but when I told him my name, he said, "Big Steve? What the fuck are you doing here?" "Remember when your partner fired me? Well I'm back."

The club was doing poorly, and Mike and Al were looking to ease their way out. They were getting older, and didn't want to put the necessary effort into turning Tuxedo around - they had a lot of other businesses that didn't require as much attention that they could focus on. They were only looking to sell 49.4% of the club at first - Mike's share - and retain majority control, with the possibility that a prospective buyer might purchase the remaining 50.6% a couple years down the line if everything went well. They were hesitant to get into business with me. I was a young kid looking to get into the game - to them, this had both positives and negatives. On one hand, I could bring a youthful energy that Tuxedo badly needed, and utilize the recent invention of social media to bring a new crowd. On the other hand, I would have been the youngest club owner in Connecticut at 29 - a potential hazard - and they had already fired me once. They turned me down, but the disappointment I felt would be short-lived.

After a few months, I received a phone call. I may not have been the perfect partner they wanted, but there weren't many other options. There just aren't a lot of people with the money and desire to buy a nightclub in central Connecticut. Mike and Al wanted to see my business plan, and I worked my ass off writing it up, hoping to get the deal done as fast as I could before the opportunity slipped away. I took the money I had made at the strip clubs and from selling coke, as well as the generous contributions of my parents, and made a significant offer. The guys accepted it, and we got started ironing out the various complex legal details involved in such a major trans-action. Every situation was considered and prepared for. One good example - the liquor license would be put under my mother's name, so that it wouldn't need to be transferred when I bought the remainder of the club, and as a precautionary measure. She was an upstanding citizen - we didn't have to worry about her going to jail or being shot in the streets, and if anything were to happen to me, she was someone I could trust 100%, and would have significant pull in the business as long as her name was on the license. Our respective attorneys went back and forth, and eventually they gave their approval.

We signed the contracts in a big, fancy legal office in Danbury and celebrated with non-alcoholic cham-pagne, along with my mother and father. Speeches were made - my mother told Al and Mike that there was only one thing she wanted from them - to not let me get killed. I stood up, and in front of everyone, I said that I wanted three things: to have sex, make money, and do cocaine. If they were ok with that, we could do good business together. I guess they were - it was official. Big Steve was now the part-owner of Tuxedo Junction, the place where it had all started. The premonition I made that day in Mike's office had come true. What are the odds? Strange things happen in life, but we have to embrace them. And I did.

CHAPTER 13

As another step into this new stage of my life, I bought a condo in Brookfield, CT that would serve as my home base. Because of the crazy hours I would be working, Julian would go back and forth between my parents' house and mine as necessary, which couldn't have been more perfect. They loved him and loved watching him grow up, and I knew he was going to be taken care of when I couldn't be there. With home life settled, I got to work. For the first year I would remain in the background at Tuxedo. Al and Mike thought a young, hotshot new owner would scare off some of the customer base they had built up, and wanted things kept hush-hush while I learned the real ins and outs of the business.

I couldn't have dreamed of two better people to

learn from - Mike and Al were serious fucking guys. All I'll say is, they were Italians from Yonkers, and they knew how shit really worked. They were millionaires with countless years of experience at countless different spots, flew in girls from Vegas, associated with guys like Frank Sinatra and other Italian gentlemen - if you get what I'm saying. When I was growing up, guys thought they were badass if they stole a Honda Accord - Mike and Al knew the kind of guys that stole excavators and dump trucks, and wouldn't get out of bed for less than a quarter of a million dollars. They had relationships with law enforcement, politicians, wealthy businessmen. They had money, and they had power. That's who I wanted to be, and I did everything I could to learn from and emulate them from the day we signed the contracts.

Mike had been the face of the nightclub, a former music manager with a big personality and a big gut, always smoking a cigar, telling stories, and schmoozing with the customers and the acts he brought in through old friendships. Al was skinny, gray-haired and more reserved, and he was the one that operated behind the scenes, dealing with the money and paperwork and working political relationships. It was Mike's stake I bought, and eventually I would be taking over his role as the face of the club, but he still owned 25% and was semi-present to oversee the transition and help me along. In the beginning, Al and I were there full time, and we spoke with Mike on a weekly basis as I started to wet my feet and learn the real ins and outs of the business.

Even though I had spent years as a bouncer and manager and knew a lot about running a club, there was even more to learn. The guys taught me how to pay employees in savvy ways to minimize loss, they taught me about things like liability, insurance claims, polygraph tests, how to beat a court case, all kinds of crazy shit you might get into, and how to get out of it. How to bend, but not break, the law, how to work within that hazy gray area that nightclub owners populate, how to keep the money coming and keep things running smoothly while protecting myself at the same time. What to watch for when moving through the space, how to prepare for every possibility, which red flags to be on the lookout for. Mike taught me about building relationships with talent, managers, agents and entertainment companies, Al did the same but with cops, city council members and judges.

One example: in Danbury, cops got $500 per hour overtime for sitting outside nightclub spots and keeping an eye on things. Because we were one of three clubs on the block, the cops would congregate nearby, and this had both benefits and positives for our business. They served as a deterrent for illegal activity outside, but some weren't cool with things going on inside. Hypothetically, if we wanted to do something that required a friendly officer who would turn a blind eye, we would need to form a relationship with the guy in charge, who could notify us when those certain friendly cops were going on duty. This was a complicated process that felt unnecessary to me, and I thought I had a better idea.

That system that the city put in place, offering cops overtime to work nightlife when they weren't on duty, was a sweet deal for the cops - they'd park their cars, sit back and make an easy extra $2500. But that money came from the taxpayers, and amounted to millions over the years. I suggested making a public effort to create a new law that would require each club to hire its own off-duty officer out of their own pocket. It would save the city tons of money, and we would be able to choose which cops worked our club. But I was naive, and Al knew better. He told me that if I messed with the cops' ability to make money, it would make me, and the club, a target, and they would try to fuck me every chance they got. Steve's got a nice car, let's pull him over and jam his ass up. The music in the club sounds a little loud, let's write him a ticket. A real businessman knows how to keep everybody happy and keep incentives aligned. This was only one part of the complicated balancing act that Mike and Al performed every day, and that I was slowly learning.

It was all new to me, but it felt natural. It was a perfect culmination of everything I had been through and everything that made me who I am. The college boy smarts instilled in me by my mother and father, the street smarts I got in Colombia and out in the world as an adult - they were always inside of me, but I hadn't put it all together until I bought the club. Mike and Al were a perfect representation of the synthesis of these parts of me. I knew the legitimate world of my parents, and the underworld I had discovered on my own - but they knew how to operate in both of these places at the same time, crossing between them and blurring the lines effortlessly. Working under them helped me understand this and turned me into the beast I am now.

My mother had some reservations - she soon realized that there were shady aspects of the nightclub business, that there were things going on under the table and behind the scenes that we would never know about, that not everything was going to be on the books. She was straight-laced, dotted every I and crossed every T, this was a strange, dark world to her - but not to me. This was my world, and I dove right in and didn't look back.

After that first year in the shadows, I started to

make myself known as the owner of Tuxedo. A lot of customers were surprised at first - they had seen me around, and I had gotten to know some of them, but they had no idea they were talking to the guy that owned the place. Now the word was out, and I began to spread my wings. There was one big change that I envisioned when I was writing my initial business plan, and I got to work on turning it into a reality. Tuxedo Junction was a large venue that required a lot of money just to open the doors. There was a secondary space, known as Club Icon, that was more of a standard nightclub, but the two were connected and had the same staff, music, entrance and the same customers - it was basically just another big room with a bar that people could walk into. But it was dirty, worn down, and wasn't bringing in much revenue. As I always did in life, I wanted more, and saw greater things.

It was my idea to use some of the cash I put into the club to renovate the building and turn Club Icon into Club Lush, a totally separate and distinct venue from Tuxedo Junction, with its own entrance, clientele, music and staff. This would allow us to create an entirely new stream of income and minimize overhead - it cost over $1000 a night to open the door at Tuxedo, and I envisioned Club Lush as a place where we could keep the party going 7 days a week while saving money on staff, air conditioning, and other expenses. We came up with a clever plan for the renovations. First, we turned Club Icon into Club Lush, and kept Tuxedo open in the meantime, then we closed Tuxedo for renovations and kept things popping at Lush until the entire process was complete, so money would always be coming in.

CHAPTER 14

Everything went smooth - the renovations were beautifully done, and Lush became my baby. I got to work turning it into the hotspot I envisioned when I first stepped into my ownership role. At that time, the industry was going through big changes. Hyped up, well-marketed parties that required tickets bought in advance or at the door were the hot new thing in nightlife, spurred on by the emergence of something called Facebook. The liquor sales that had always been so profitable were on the downswing, and cost of entry was a new and suddenly necessary stream of income. These parties were usually put on by promoters, new figures in the industry, and advertised on social media and via word of mouth. They had to be cool, exciting, exclusive, they had to pop. Navigating this unfamiliar world would have been impossible for old-school guys like Mike and Al. They didn't know how to use Facebook or deal with the coked-out, bratty promoters. They couldn't chat outside the clubs with the young customers - imagine 60 year old guys in suits chatting it up with college kids. But I was still in my twenties, and I could do it all, and better than anyone. They had expected me to bring this youthful edge, and I exceeded their expectations.

Thursdays were always college nights, and they drew big crowds that filled Tuxedo to the brim. Fridays they had contemporary music and those were also successful nights, but it was a more subdued, white crowd. Saturdays and Sundays had been slow for some time, and I decided to bring in a new kind of urban clientele that fit my own personality. Saturdays would be rap and hip-hop, and Sundays would be Brazilian nights. I befriended local kids from the projects that helped me spread the word in exchange for free drinks, and soon Saturdays and Sundays became our most lucrative nights.

I was the man - I was young, handsome, fit, I had money, and I owned two of the hottest clubs in town. Guys wanted to be me, and girls wanted to fuck me - and there was always an endless stream of them walking through my doors. I was surrounded by people that wanted to get to know me every night. But with success, especially in the nightclub business, comes a type of danger that requires total preparation and awareness to circumvent. A lot of the friends I made then weren't real friends - something that became even more clear to me years later - and amongst them were drug dealers, street kids, legitimate gangsters, scammers, robbers. People that you're never truly safe around. I was fortunate to have been steered in a safe direction by my parents, as well as my co-owners, and they taught me how to protect myself from any situation I might find myself in.

Every night I'd bring some people back to my place for after hours parties, including whichever girl I would be taking to bed. But never my real home, never the place I truly rested my head - my condo in Brookfield was my sanctuary, a 3-store luxury home in a gated community down the street from the Governor's house, my seclusion away from the underworld. I had been instructed to always have a sparsely furnished backup apartment for things like partying and hooking up with girls, to never bring anyone around my house, where my expensive shit might get stolen, where certain people might be waiting the following day to rob me or worse. My success was necessarily public - I had to be out there, with nice cars, nice clothes, nice watches, I had to sell the lifestyle - but it made me a target. I always carried a gun on me, and even if I were caught off-guard, other precautions had been taken. My house, my cars, the businesses, they were always put in someone else's name, so that if someone did have a gun to my head, they would never be able to access the real money.

Despite the dangers, things were good. The money was rolling in, I was exceeding expectations at work, I was partying, I was hooking up with girls, I was doing cocaine - everything I had promised at that lawyer's office two years before. Even family life was going well. My brother Mike bought a gym, and I helped him manage it during the day. My parents and I were loving the experience of raising Julian together, and he couldn't have been happier and healthier.

One night, I spotted a woman on the porch at Club Lush, and I knew immediately that I had to get to know her. She stood out, even amongst the many beautiful women that were always hanging around. She was different, a little older, something in her eyes and the way she carried herself, she was distinct even in the crowd, curvy, gorgeous, Latina - my kind of woman. I introduced myself and told her I needed to know who she is. Her name was Carmen, and she told me that her brother worked for me as a bouncer, and we talked, and got to know each other, and soon we were fucking regularly, she would visit me and I would visit her. I liked that she had her own place and her own car, that she knew how to cook and clean, that she was grown. It wasn't long before she told me she was pregnant.

My mother and father were upset that I was already having another kid, with a new woman that I barely knew, but Carmen and I decided to keep the child and our lives became intertwined. She was living in a bad area in Waterbury, and I moved her into a nice house in Bethel where she would be safe and comfortable for the pregnancy. Our relationship became fully formed, but just as they had with Amanda, problems started to surface soon after. I found out that Carmen lived on Section 8, and wasn't as independent as I had first thought, and that she would need to lean on me like any of the others girls I had been fucking with. There were also major personality conflicts. Like Amanda, Carmen had lived a rough and impoverished life. In my family, we resolved conflicts calmly and respectfully, and this is what I expected in my serious romantic relationships, but in Carmen's family, it was common to have explosive, even violent fights, and this is what began to take place between us. Her family was a problem in itself - she had several brothers, including the one that worked for me, and she was always running to them whenever we got into a fight. They would make a big scene of showing up, threatening me, getting involved in things they shouldn't have been - childish shit, shit that I didn't want to deal with.

If I was going to make it work with Carmen, I was going to have to make it work with her family, and I tried. One brother was an aspiring rapper, and I helped him make some connections in the business through some of my own I made at the club. Another brother wanted to work in construction, and I hooked him up with a nice gig with some friends of mine. But she had another brother who didn't have such innocent career goals. He was a serious gangster, known for violent robberies and kidnappings. Carmen herself had been kidnapped by one of his associates, thrown into a trunk and driven halfway to Brooklyn where she probably would have been killed if the police hadn't found her. It was dangerous shit, shit that a man in my position should never be involved with.

Al taught me that in the hazy gray legal area we inhabited, I would come across certain people, low-level people, that will do the most risky, illegal shit, with little to gain because they have little or nothing to lose. The real intelligent businessmen will hire those people to do their dirty work, but will never get too close, always hovering above the real violence and filth so that they can keep themselves clean. As soon as I might identify these individuals, I must separate myself from them as quickly and as definitively as possible - unlike them, I have something to lose. I can't give details, but after one situation at Carmen's family's house that involved a shooting, that's exactly what I did - separate myself from them. With her brothers more or less out of the picture - at least my picture - Carmen and I were able to continue working on our relationship as her belly began to grow.

CHAPTER 15

Some months after things were settled with Carmen and just as life had begun to resume as normal, I was working at the club when I received a phone call from my mother. "Dad's not doing too well," she said, and before she finished her sentence I was out the door and on my way to my parents' house. My father said he felt fine and didn't want to go to the hospital, but I insisted on spending the night just in case anything happened. Some hours later, my mother's screams woke me from my troubled sleep, and I ran out of the guest bedroom into theirs, where my father had collapsed onto the floor due to a massive heart attack. I checked his pulse and fear struck me when I realized that he didn't have one, and I immediately started CPR, pumping his chest and breathing air into his lungs while my mother called 911.

By the time the paramedics arrived, I had successfully restarted his heart. As they lifted him onto a stretcher, they told me that it seemed he had also suffered a stroke as a result of the emergency resuscitation. He was rushed to the hospital, where he was placed in critical care, and we feared he would not survive the night, my mother hysterical and I in total shock. When the dust settled, we were informed that he was in a coma, and that it didn't look good but they would do everything they could to bring him back to us. After a few days by his side, I decided it would be best to resume living my life - there wasn't anything I could do, and it was difficult to see him in that state.

For a few weeks I tried distracting myself with work, with family, with my young son and my unborn child that would be arriving soon, but my father's condition did not improve, and the sense of impending doom that had begun to creep over me on the night of my mother's phone call soon enveloped me totally. Doctors told us that my father had a rare lung condition, that he was essentially brain dead, that he was a vegetable and though he could be kept alive, he would remain in that state for the rest of his life, if one can even call that life. At first I resisted, then stalled, grasping onto some kind of impossible hope that things would change, that the doctors were wrong, grasping onto a miraculous possibility that would never come, but soon it became clear that a decision would have to be made, and I would have to be the one to make it.

We had discussions, my mother and I, difficult discussions that you have when the life of a loved one has been unexpectedly placed into your hands. If he was kept alive, we would be able to hold onto that optimism, the chance for a miracle - but we knew by that time that those hopes were false, and that though his heart would be beating, and there would be air in his lungs, he would never really be alive again. And I knew my father, knew him as well as one can know a man, and I knew that he would never want to live like that - that a decision to keep him alive would in many ways be a selfish one. So we gathered around, we said our goodbyes, and we held him until his last breath. And then he was gone.

I was devastated. My birth father was killed, the rest of my biological family murdered in front of me, and now I had watched as the man who raised me in his arms died in mine only a few weeks after I saved his life. And he saved mine, many times in many ways in all the years that had passed since we locked eyes on the playground at the orphanage. I love my mother, and she loved me, but on two separate occasions she wanted to give me up, to send me back to that orphanage, to Colombia, to give up on me - but my father resisted. "He just needs love," he told her, again and again over the years as I struggled to adapt and struggled to fit in. If he never said those words, I would not be writing this now - I'd be running a Cartel or I would already be dead.

He gave me everything - the moral compass that I hold so dear and which steers me in the right direction every day, my first dirt bike, my first gun, my first nightclub. He taught me how to be a father, to go after my dreams, to be more and to be better. He had always been there for me from our first day together, the gentle hand on my back that guided me through the alien world of JFK airport and beyond, that guided me throughout my entire life. Without that, what was I going to do? It was the most difficult thing I had ever been through, and I took it hard.

Julian took it even harder. He was only 3 years old, but my father and him had grown extraordinarily close. He lost his papa, his best friend, who helped raise him, who fed him and changed his diapers - he was distraught. It also took a real toll on my brother Mike, and on my mother - we were all destroyed by the sudden loss of the man we loved, who had kept our family together. But there wasn't much time to wallow in grief, however painful and overpowering it may have been. A vacuum had appeared in the wake of my father's death, not only in our lives, but in the managing of our family's various financial interests, and someone needed to step up and fill it.

Al and I had become very close in the two years since I got into business with him, but our conversations were usually business-related or lighthearted. After my father's passing, I began to look to him as a kind of father-figure, someone that I could talk to about life, that I respected and that I could trust to point me in the right direction. I told Al in the weeks after the funeral about the mess my father had left behind - the businesses, the real estate investments, the money that was tied up in the stock market. How were we supposed to handle it all? My mother and brother weren't equipped to take over, but I had one kid, another on the way, two nightclubs, a crazy relationship - it couldn't all fall on me, right? Al wouldn't hear any of it - to him, they were excuses, and a grown man with a family and responsibilities doesn't have the luxury of making excuses. He told me that I had to step up, and fast - there was no time for self-pity. My family needed me - was I going to be a man and do what had to be done? I took his advice, and began handling things on my own, more than I should have, but as much as I had to to keep everything in order. We were all devastated, but as had always been the case, Mike and I processed emotions differently. His pressed inward and caused him to retreat into himself, to draw himself away - mine pushed outward and forward into the world and into action. In the past, this may have caused bad behavior, but as a grown man, this allowed me to carry this new load on my back, along with the others that had piled up over the years.

CHAPTER 16

With our family affairs straightened out, I brought that energy with me back to Tuxedo Junction and Club Lush. My father had taught me to go after my dreams and make them a reality, and though things were going well at the clubs, I wanted more and I was going to get it - for him, for my kids, for Al, and for myself. I decided to shake things up, and I set my sights on the model of throwing parties with promoters that had become industry standard. Promoters were third-party figures that would book an act and advertise a party via social media, flyers and word-of-mouth and supply bodies, bodies that bought drinks. In exchange for that service, they were paid the lion's share of ticket sales at the door. But liquor sales continued to decline, and I didn't like that this new source of revenue was going straight into pockets that weren't mine. I decided I would cut out the middle man. I had all of the skills, knowledge and connections that promoters had, times a million. I knew how to book acts, how to use Facebook, and I had a lot of relationships with people around town that would help me hype things up through word-of-mouth. Big Steve was going to throw a big party, his very own - but first, I would need a big act.

I got in touch with a guy named DJ Toro, who was managing the rapper Cassidy at the time. Cassidy had just beat a murder case, and was looking to get back in the game. We did the whole deal over the phone, no contracts or nothing - $1500 up front, and $1500 the night of the party. I hired a local DJ from Danbury, DJ Jerry, to provide music and help me promote the event. It was a huge success - we packed the club, Cassidy gave a great performance, and we made a killing. I celebrated late into the night, then fell into a deep, happy sleep.

That sleep was cut short by a phone call from Carmen - the baby was coming. I picked her up and we sped over to the hospital. The hazy numbness I experienced during the birth of my first son had been replaced by a rush of excitement. In the three years that passed between their arrivals, I turned my life around. There was so much going on. The good - the clubs, my health - and the bad - the recent passing of my father, and the extra load of responsibility I took on in its wake. It was a crazy time to welcome another child, but they come when they're ready, and I was happy despite everything happening around us. Everything went well, and Carmen gave birth comfortably to a healthy little boy that we named Julius. I brought something special to the hospital to celebrate - a fat wad of cash. I covered him in the pile of bills and took a photo to capture the moment. It was a wonderful day, only saddened somewhat by the fact that my father wasn't there to meet his new grandson.

Me and infant Julius, who we nicknamed "Bebe".

Around this time, we sold my parents' house, and I moved my mother into a luxury home in Fairfield. Julian was in a nice private pre-school by then, and he continued to go back and forth between my mother and I. I also moved Carmen and Julius into a house where they would have more room, and I started to spend most of my time there so that we could establish ourselves as a family. In the months since Carmen had become pregnant, I had made a concerted effort to work on our relationship, but little progress was made. She had certain expectations of a partner that a man in the nightclub industry like myself would never be able to live up to, and she became more and more aware of this as time passed. Coming home at dawn was normal for me, that was just when my work day ended, but when I was staying with her, she saw this as an act of outright disrespect. She'd wait up for me and start yelling as soon as I walked through the door. It was a headache, one that I felt I didn't deserve considering that I was the one paying for everything, and this was how I did it.

But that's how she handled every conflict, both minor and major. Screaming, cursing, causing a big scene. Carmen was raised in survival mode, around criminals, scammers, and the chaos of poverty, and everything was life or death. The irony was, I had really come from a similar background in Colombia, and maybe this is what drew us together at first. She was fiery and passionate, and I liked that about her, but when you first fall in love with someone, when you're in that honeymoon stage, you have blinders on. When you're pushed closer together, especially in the way that having a child together does, another side to them might reveal itself.

Carmen didn't like my lifestyle - the late nights, the parties, the drugs, the alcohol, the violence - she thought her man should live a respectable life, and exist within the boundaries that she herself set. She was deeply jealous of the beautiful women that worked for me, which became a real problem at home and at work. There was one bartender that worked on Sundays at Brazilian nights that I previously had a fling with. Carmen was so upset that I would be spending time with this girl, that I gave up working on Sundays just to placate her. I told Al that if he took over Brazilian nights by himself, I would take sole responsibility of Saturdays, busy nights that always required both of us to be present, so that he could spend time with his wife. I probably lost out on hundreds of thousands of dollars by giving up those Sundays, all to make Carmen feel better. Al taught me later that with women, you either tell them everything or you tell them nothing, never in between, and in between was exactly where I got stuck.

I tried everything I could to be a good partner and father, but nothing worked. Carmen was gorgeous, she cooked, she cleaned, we had great sex to the end, but we just weren't a good match. The fighting was incessant and I didn't see any way to move forward together. A few months after Julius was born, I told Carmen that I was leaving her. As I could have predicted, she was furious. She was so mad, she decided to keep Julius away from me, refusing to let me see him. I was angry, but what was I supposed to do? Fighting her would only cause more headaches, more explosive fighting that would have a damaging effect on my infant child. It could even turn dangerous, as it had with Amanda. I turned the other cheek and went back to work. Months went by - I missed Julius' first steps, his first bites of food, his first words, memories I can never get back.

My mother sat me down for a frank discussion about the women I was attracting and choosing to spend my time with. She observed that the girls I had kids with were both extremely damaged and troubled, which only brought chaos and heartbreak into my life, and that I met them and my many other casual hookups exclusively at my clubs or any other place a party was happening. She told me that this wasn't the way to find a good woman, that flashing my money, jewelry, cars and lifestyle as a good-looking young guy would draw attention from the wrong kind of people who are only interested in getting things from me, rather than being with me truly. In my own way, in my little pond of Danbury, Connecticut, I was a big fish, a superstar - how does a superstar know who really loves them, who really has their best intentions at heart? It takes maturity and awareness, and these are the things my mother stressed during this tumultuous period. It helped me change my mindset as I pressed forward.

A few months after Carmen and I broke up, she started to allow me to visit her and Julius, and we established a civil, workable co-parenting relationship. Finally, I was able to see and spend time with both of my kids, and we all started to come together as a family.

Me and my boys.

Once I got into the rhythm of this new life, with its many new elements, I turned my attention back to work. My first party had been a big success, and in the following months I capitalized on it. By this time, I had solidified a consistent party at Club Lush every Saturday night, and one big one per month at Tuxedo Junction, under my own name. The new stream of revenue coming in from ticket sales at the door was a boon for our business and my pockets. We also rented the club out, which was another good source of income, and also provided me with one encounter that I'll never forget.

One day, Al and I were chilling in the back office when we noticed, on our live security feed, a brand new black Chevy Tahoe pulling right up to the front door of the club. This got our attention - most people parked in the lot and walked inside - and our curiosity increased when we saw who was inside. The driver, a big black guy, got out and opened the rear door - two short Italian guys, impeccably dressed with fancy suits and pinky rings, hopped out, followed by another burly bodyguard. We didn't know who it was, but we knew it was someone. They knocked on the closed door, our security answered, and one of the guys, who seemed to be in charge, said he was looking for Big Steve. I gave them the OK to bring these strangers back to our office, and my security team escorted them to the door. The two short guys walked in, leaving their bodyguards outside - I remember, before the door closed, thinking that it was like a showdown, between their bodyguards and our security, facing each other, sizing each other up, all trained and ready if some shit were to go down.

That tension carried over into the office, and it was so thick you could cut it with a knife. There was *something* about these guys, something indescribable about the way they carried themselves - you could tell they were important, that they were serious fucking guys not to be messed with. The guy in charge looked so familiar, but I couldn't place him until he introduced himself as Al Capone's grandson. You read books, watch movies and hear stories about guys like this, but you don't really get it until you're in the room with one of them. He may not have been as famous or powerful as his grandfather, but he looked identical to him, and he possessed an intimidating gravitas that I had never experienced before. One of his partners owned an entertainment company, and they wanted to rent out Tuxedo for a big party featuring a reggaeton artist they were working with. Ultimately, the party wasn't too successful, but I stayed in touch with him and some of his associates and we did some good business together.

CHAPTER 17

I was in touch with a lot of people in the entertainment industry then. By that time, talent managers and agents were reaching out to me directly to make deals and get their artists gigs at my clubs. We had a lot of big acts come through our doors, including Red Cafe and Lloyd Banks, fresh off his big hit "Beamer, Benz, or Bentley" which he performed to a rocking, sold out crowd. But the most famous artist we ever booked, for what would become our most profitable night of my entire run, didn't even end up performing. Meek Mill was an up and coming rapper that had just signed a deal with Rick Ross and his label MMG. I was becoming friendly with a music industry player named Big Mike, and he hooked me up with Meek's people and I was able to book Meek for one night at Tuxedo. This would be our biggest party ever, and I went all out promoting and marketing the shit out of it, by any means necessary.

We packed the club with over 1000 people, all clamoring to see Meek on stage. I thought it was going to be a great night - then things turned ugly. When you have that many people, especially people from the hood like we did, all stuffed together in a space that's not meant to fit them, hyped up to see a big rapper, with loud music, drinks, drugs all getting them more and more excited, it only takes a little spark for things to blow up in a big, dangerous way. Before Meek even took the stage, a fight broke out - small at first, but as bodies collided and errant punches and cocktail glasses struck uninvolved bystanders, it rapidly expanded. Before long, that little fight had exploded into a full blown riot. Connecticut State Police descended on the club and the officers were forced to pepper spray and beat our customers with batons in order to put an end to the chaos. They shut the club down for the remainder of the night, and Meek never performed. The silver lining: we made over $30,000 that night.

It was crazy, and it's a bad look to have your guests pepper-sprayed and beaten, but to me, this was just another night of running a nightclub. You never knew what was going to go down, and you had to roll with it. But other people didn't see it like that. The mayor of Danbury at the time was a conservative, clean-cut guy that didn't care for nightlife and the kind of people it drew to his wealthy, whitebred town. He saw the Meek Mill riot as something he could use to push his own agenda, and he took full advantage. He wrote an article in the local paper about the club that heavily criticized us and our handling of the party, as well as what he saw as other transgressions we had been guilty of in the past. I wanted to respond publicly to the article, but Al convinced me otherwise - it was better not to draw more attention to ourselves.

The riot and the mayor's article got a lot of public attention, and he used this momentum to create a totally new taskforce dedicated to observing and reporting on nightlife venues in town. I was going to a lot of public meetings, such as City Council meetings, throughout my time owning the clubs as suggested by Al - it was an important part of the business, though I thought my time would've been better spent doing coke and fucking girls - and I got the entire troubling picture. This would be funded with taxpayer money and, naturally, led by one of the mayor's closest friends. The guys they hired as part of the new task-force drove around in brand-new, unmarked vehicles and were always ready to write us a ticket for the smallest possible infraction, even something as stupid as cigarette butts littered on the sidewalk outside.

They weren't police, but they were affiliated with them and had much of the same power over us as real cops. They had the authority to fine nightclubs like ours thousands and thousands of dollars, and really became pains in our asses. Weren't there more important things that this much taxpayer money could be spent on, things that would be more helpful to the town than a bunch of rent-a-cop hall monitors?

The riot and the ensuing backlash it caused proved to be a dark omen of what was to come. By the third and fourth years of my ownership tenure, business was booming, but as the number of customers coming through our door and the number of drinks sold increased, so did the number of dangerous legal problems we faced on what seemed like a weekly basis. A nightclub is a living, breathing liability for its owners, and I had two of them. Every night brought the titillating potential for a big payoff as well as a cataclysmic emergency that could jam me up for months or even years. The balancing act required to navigate the risk-reward proposition of nightclub ownership was becoming more and more difficult for me to perform, and on several occasions I was pushed to the brink of financial and legal ruin.

One night, a young blonde girl from New York was sitting on the railing of our second floor balcony, having a good time, when she slipped off and cracked her head open on the ground below. To make matters worse, she was underage and had gotten drunk at our bar. Her father was a sergeant with the NYPD, and he smelled blood and money and went after us like a rabid dog. He had the knowledge and connections to really fuck us, but Al knew how to deal with men that have power. We did a little research of our own, made some calls, asked the right questions, and discovered that she snuck into the club - not illegally granted entry by our bouncers - and that she had drugs in her system on the night of her fall. Sergeant Daddy didn't want to face the embarrassment of his daughter's drug use and underage partying going public, and the criminal charges and civil lawsuits we faced were quickly and quietly swept under the rug.

Just as one crisis is averted, another emerges, as it did the day we were raided by a team of ATF agents. There was a guy, let's call him T, who had been my top bouncer, and became something of a manager that helped me run Club Lush on a day-to-day basis. Unbeknownst to me, he was running something else under our roof - a marijuana trafficking business. He was distributing pounds and pounds of the shit out of my club. I was furious, but he was of such vital importance to the operations of the club that I knew I had to do what I could to keep him working for us. Some phone calls were made to the right individuals, and T was let off with a stern warning and served no jail time.

There were plenty of smaller problems to deal with in between those more major events. There were nightly fistfights taking place in the clubs, most often on Saturday nights when we had an urban crowd full of people from the local projects. Kids had beef on the streets, and they took it inside our doors, where it came to a head and often exploded amidst the flowing drinks, banging rap music, and assorted recreational drugs that were always around. My security team was good, but it was impossible to totally prevent these incidents of random violence - it was just something we had to live with. But I did come up with an idea that I thought might help limit fights during our business hours and also make me some extra cash. I organized twice-weekly fightclubs at Tuxedo Junction that took place after we shut down for the night. Kids from rival projects that had beef with one another took their shirts off and had it out in front of the big crowd that would gather to watch and place bets on the action, bets I was more than happy to take and pocket the vig on. These were usually the same kids that would get in fights at the club anyway, and because I gave them a space to settle their problems and have fun in a somewhat controlled environment, they paid me and the club respect by waiting until after hours to fuck each other up.

The constant headaches involved in nightclub ownership were starting to wear on me. It had been four years since I bought Tuxedo Junction and Club Lush, and I brought a lot of success with me during that time, but I was beginning to fall out of love with it. I was getting older, and the lifestyle wasn't as fresh and exciting as it had been in those early days. It became strictly business to me, and it was a difficult and even dangerous business. I also began to feel an urge deep inside of me to look to the future, to tackle some new challenge, venture into a new industry, start a new business - that hustler mindset that was always with me. I had accomplished a lot of what I wanted in the nightlife industry, and didn't feel the passion for it that I once did. But before I could even begin thinking about my next move, I would need to find a successor, someone to pass the torch to as Al and Mike passed it to me, to carry on the legacy, to innovate, to bring new energy into the clubs I had poured so much of my blood, money and spirit into. It didn't take long for him to appear.

CHAPTER 18

I noticed that under 18 parties were becoming popular in the industry again, but there weren't any spots in Danbury hosting these events yet, and I decided to take advantage. These were parties for underage kids where no alcohol was served - kind of like a school dance but in a real nightlife venue. A promoter that knew how to appeal to the teen demographic was hired to advertise and sell tickets, and we made our money renting out the space and selling bottled water, juices and Red Bulls at the bar. They were low-risk, low-overhead, and at first, low-reward. They were doing alright, we pulled decent crowds and made decent money, but nothing I would call a major success. There was no hype, no buzz leading up to the events, resulting in flat, unexciting nights rather than the big bangs that I always went for. I thought that the promoters and other individuals that were organizing them were doing a subpar job. I wasn't the only one.

During one of these teen parties, I happened to be on the premises, and was making my rounds when I was approached by a snot-nosed little whiteboy - later, I would find out that he was 15, but he didn't look a day over 12. With a level of confidence that some grown men can only dream of, he looked me dead in the eyes and told me that he could throw a better party himself. His name was Ian Bick, and I quickly began to like him. Something about him - he had charisma, he had big dreams, big ideas, he was a hustler - he reminded me a little of myself. And he was a great talker - he could talk anybody into anything. Eventually, it would be those skills that would be his - and nearly my own - downfall, but at that time, I bought it. I told him that if he could get the $1500 that it cost to rent the club for the night, he could have a party of his own. He took the opportunity and ran with it.

A few weeks later, it was Ian's big night, his chance to prove himself. When I pulled up to the club and saw what he had done, my jaw dropped - there were hundreds and hundreds of kids lined up around the block. He had pulled more bodies than we managed at some of our rap parties with major artists. In the weeks leading up to that night, he had promoted the party better than anyone I had ever seen. He had a natural talent for marketing, elite social media skills, and an innate understanding of his target demographic, all of which he took full advantage of. The party was a massive success - collectively, we made tens of thousands of dollars that night. Al and I were pleasantly surprised by the turnout, and we decided to continue working with Ian as we mentored him in the ways of the business.

We started doing parties with Ian every month or so, and it quickly became clear that he was a prodigy. Making connections, marketing, building hype, it all came easily to him - it was like he was born for it. By his third or fourth party, every kid in the area knew his name and wanted to be at his next big bash. Al and I watched with genuine awe as each event became more successful than the last. He had figured out how to build a brand for himself before anyone knew what a brand was, and managed to turn himself into a local celebrity. Money was coming in, a lot for a grown man but for a 16 year old kid it was insane. He made us a lot of money as well, and we did some great business together in the year, year and a half of monthly teen parties, all headlined by the name that had become a guaranteed profit - Ian Bick.

He was young, too young, but I started to believe I had found the protege I was looking for, the next big thing in nightlife. Someone that knows the crowd because he is the crowd, someone that's right there in the middle of it, living it and learning it every day. In the past, a kid like him would have had to start from the bottom and work his way up, regardless of talent. But the emergence of social media had ushered in a wild new world, where anyone could be anything as long as it said so on their Facebook page. A 16 year old kid could be a chef, a director, a day trader, or in Ian's case - a club promoter. The eyes of everyone in your town, everyone in your county, everyone in the world were right there, on your phone or laptop, in your house, to look at whatever you were selling, for free and with the click of a button - if you knew how to work it. And Ian knew how to work it. Even in this new world, the rules of the old still applied - if you can make me money, we can do business together, whether you're 5 years old or 105.

In that honeymoon phase of working with Ian, we saw a lot of promise in him, and in some ways we were already grooming him as a potential successor. We were trying to push him in the right direction, teaching him not only the ways of the nightclub world but how to handle his own finances and personal businesses as well. But as Ian's star and pockets grew, so did his ego and ambitions, and I watched as he began to change into something bigger than Al and I could handle. I realize now that it was never really about the money to Ian, at least not the legitimate businessman's kind of money that I had learned from my parents, Al and Mike. He was so young and so successful, I'm sure he thought that it would always be coming in, and didn't concern himself with exact numbers, with budgeting, with planning for the future and protecting himself. He was really interested in building his minor celebrity, making friends with rappers, with the guys that wanted to be him and, even more so, the girls that wanted to fuck him. With vacations and shiny things to show off around town - he wanted to feel like a big shot, like a super-star. I can't blame him - everyone wants to feel like that, myself included, and he was a fucking kid. But he had the potential for greatness, for big things, and those things take patience, planning and serious consideration. Al and I tried to instill this in him, but he didn't listen. Just as I always had, he wanted more, and he was going to get it by any means necessary.

About two years after I had first met Ian, he had outgrown teen parties along with the rest of his peers. Truthfully, even 16 is a little old for under-18 events - a lot of kids are drinking and doing drugs by that age - and by 18 they're considered extremely uncool. Now, instead of marketing to people his own age, he was a 17 year old targeting 13 and 14 year olds, and all the new friends he made in his rise to stardom had lost interest in his parties. This is a crucial difference between Ian and the older people that threw underage parties. They found a niche, and they stuck with it - they weren't friends with the kids that went to the parties, their identities weren't tied to being popular with that crowd, they didn't have to enjoy the parties themselves. It was just a business to them. For Ian, it was his whole world, and as he got older, his interests changed as they do with all teenagers. Him and his friends wanted to go to mature parties, with drugs, with alcohol, with big rappers and college kids, that's what they thought was cool and exciting, as they once thought of the teen parties but no longer did. And so these are the kinds of parties that Ian was beginning to want to throw himself.

Al and I advised strongly against this. He was too young - he didn't understand the 21 and over demographic like he did the under 18. How could he? He was still only 17 himself. And the teen parties were simple and low-risk - there was only so much money he could lose in a night, the cost of renting out the club and hiring a DJ. 21+ events are much more complex and can be much more expensive. You need different kinds of security, insurance. You might want to hire a big artist that carries with him a big fee that must be paid regardless of how many tickets you sell, and you might need a bigger venue to accommodate that artist. These are all additional expenses that amount to greater risk for the promoter than what Ian took on with his teen parties. But because he had never had an unsuccessful party, he never considered those risks, even though they would grow exponentially along with his new ambitions. Everything had come so easily to him at first, he never stopped to think about what might happen if he failed - it just never entered his mind. We warned him to stay in his lane. He had a great thing going, and he was still a kid. All he needed was to have some patience, to not get too ahead of himself, and the world was his. But he wasn't hearing any of it.

CHAPTER 19

I t was the spring of 2012, the end of his junior year of high school, when Ian started to plan his first big 21 and over party. He had already begun to dabble in bigger events under the name of his new company This Is Where It's At, and had expanded from just working with us at Tuxedo Junction to partnering with clubs all over Connecticut - by this point he had done hundreds of parties. To help cover the cost of these larger events, he would secure investments from locals - often his friends' parents - and they would inevitably receive an impressive return on their investment after the party would turn out to be another inevitable success. That he, a high school student, was able to convince adults to invest thousands of dollars into his party promotion business shows just how skilled he was, and how well-known his exploits had become. He had taken a full step up from the small teen parties that he started with, and things were going well, but still he was unsatisfied. He wanted something huge, something that would make headlines, something that would serve as his real introduction to the world of the big boys. He saw the kinds of big rap parties that guys like myself and Big Mike were throwing in the area, and he wanted to prove he could do it bigger and better.

He set his sights on the rapper Big Sean, a rising star that had just been featured on the hit compilation album *Cruel Summer* from Kanye West's GOOD Music. Big Sean was becoming huge with the younger crowd, and Ian started negotiating with his people. A big name like Big Sean would require a big venue, and Ian chose the basketball arena at Western Connecticut State University - WestConn to us - for the occasion. Ian was working totally independently of us, but Al and I still had a strong relationship with him and we continued to try to mentor him as he stepped into this new phase of his career. The Big Sean concert would present an unprecedented risk for Ian. His fee alone would reach into the high 5 figures, and the arena at WestConn seats 8,000 people, a far cry from the 800 person venues he was accustomed to filling. We tried to steer him away from such an expensive event, but Ian saw big lights and dollar signs, and he pushed forward. Internally, I questioned how he could afford to leverage himself and his investors in the way he would have to in order to pull it all off, but there was only so much I could do - it wasn't happening under my roof, so it really wasn't my business anymore.

The concert was originally planned for the middle of the Summer of 2012, but was pushed to September. Though Ian managed to pull a decent crowd, it wasn't enough to make him a profit - in fact, he ended up losing money. I didn't know how much, but I knew that it was a lot - all in all he had probably put out over $100k, and though I wasn't there, from what I heard at the time it was a disappointing turnout. Ian couldn't relate to the 21+ crowd - he didn't know how to appeal to them like he did with kids his age and younger. It makes sense - why would a 22 year old college senior want to go to a party thrown by a 17 year old? He had a big name artist, but wasn't able to build the magical hype he once had. Though the party was a failure, Ian seemed to brush it off, and he and other people around him saw it more as a learning experience to build from than a sign that he should scale things back. But I saw it as a red flag. If Ian was such a prodigy, as we had all thought, how could this party have gone so poorly? How could he have planned so poorly, ignored all the warnings, and failed to protect himself? It was another bad omen of what was to come.

It was around this time that I started to plan my exit from the nightclub business. I took a look around, and decided that I didn't like the direction that things were going. Al had become like another father to me - he had taught me everything I knew about the business and more. On the day we signed our contracts, he made a promise to my mother that he would do everything in his power to keep me safe, and he kept that promise. I trusted him as much as I could ever trust another man. When he started to admit that he shared some of my concerns about the business and where it was headed, I started to seriously consider stepping away. We realized that what we had been doing, what had once brought us so much success, wasn't working anymore, and that a big change was needed. We talked about making major renovations to the club, but we knew that wasn't going to solve the problem. The industry itself was changing. It was becoming younger, and foreign to guys like Al and even myself - young hotshots like Ian were the next big thing, and we were old news. We even considered closing down and selling Tuxedo and Lush.

Ian's big party at WestConn had been a failure, but it hadn't stopped him, it hadn't even slowed him down. In the months that followed, he had fully expanded his business into 21+ parties, and was doing a steady stream of them at venues all over the state. Al and I still saw a lot of potential in him, and looked at him as our own protege that we helped reach unprecedented heights for a kid his age. Having such a natural successor in place helped me make the decision. After Ian graduated high school in 2013, we brought him in to help manage the club - for the next year, Al and I would groom him to take over my position as I transitioned into a new phase of my life.

Ian immediately took off running, and we let him put his own special sauce on Tuxedo Junction. It was his club now, and this is how he advertised it on his social media pages. On paper, no money had been exchanged, and I and my family remained legal owners of the clubs and the liquor licenses, but Ian made it his own as I gradually began to spend less and less time there. As we predicted, Ian was a natural fit and brought a new energy to Tuxedo that led to a spike in business. This allowed me to begin to refocus on other aspects of my life that had been neglected during my years of working nonstop hours at the clubs.

My kids were getting older, and I spent a lot of my newfound free time with them. My mother had taken on much of the responsibility of raising Julian during my years at the clubs, and I made sure to make more of an effort in his life. He was 6 years old by then, in first grade in a nice private school, and I quickly realized as I tried to put my own imprint on him that my mother's style of parenting clashed with my own - this led to some serious disputes between her and I. She was singularly focused on Julian's performance in school and making sure he was booked with extracurricular activities like sports. I felt that she had neglected other aspects of his life that had been so important to me as a kid. I wanted my son to reflect some of my style and background - I wanted him to have fresh haircuts and brand new Jordans on his feet, I wanted him to be different from all the other rich white kids he went to school with. She didn't care about any of that, and thought it was ridiculous to put time, money and effort into making him stand out. We really got into it a few times. All I wanted was a combination of everything, and at the time it pissed me off that she was turning my son into something different than I envisioned, but I realize now that she was really coming from a good place.

Julian, or Bebe as we had started to call him, was living full time with Carmen, and I visited them more often as her and I continued to work through some of our issues. Since our relationship had deteriorated I had mostly been fucking around with different girls, but around this time I got into a serious relationship with a beautiful woman named Deandra. I was doing a lot of research into what my next move might be, trying to plan for my future. In the meantime, Ian was becoming more fully ingrained in the club as my visits there became less and less frequent. By 2014, I had separated myself completely.

In the 5 years I spent as the owner of Tuxedo Junction, I had lived an entire lifetime, complete with a rise and fall arc that I felt had completed to my satisfaction by that time. I had done it all and seen it all, and I was finally ready to move on. Al was going to stay on and continue to mentor Ian as he took over my place completely. On my way out, Al told me that if there was any other kind of business I'd ever like to get into, he would be happy to have me as a partner. I would have loved to, but the kinds of businesses that Al got into required a lot of liquid cash that I didn't have. My money was tied up in real estate and in the clubs - Al's was too, but he also had untold millions in the bank that could be spent on opening new restaurants and clubs or starting new business ventures. Still, it was a generous offer, and it meant a lot to me - Al had done so much for me, and I always wanted his approval. This told me that I really had managed to get it.

CHAPTER 20

In every way but on the dotted line, Ian was now the co-owner of Tuxedo Junction and Club Lush. The only money I received was the monthly fee that Ian paid me to lease the liquor license that was still in my mother's name, for which we worked out a flat rate. This provided me with a steady stream of income and gave me some pull in the business should anything go wrong. Other than that, I had completely distanced myself. For a while, I was basically retired. I continued the search for my next big move, but nothing inspired the passion in me that nightlife did. I had been so busy tying up loose ends at the club, getting closer to my kids, and tending to family business matters, that I had failed to formulate a real plan for myself before getting out of the game. I felt lost. Every other time in my life up to this point had been a nonstop hustle - always onto bigger and better, always moving, always making deals - there was always another concert, always another party, always another rapper coming to town, and as soon as the Sun came up, the cycle started again. But that cycle had been broken, and replaced by a feeling of emptiness and lack of purpose that was difficult to shake.

I became embroiled in a legal dispute with Carmen over child support payments, and the heat it brought onto me and my books was the last thing I needed. I decided to get a straight job to show a legitimate stream of income that would help me in court. This proved to be more difficult than I had anticipated. I had a college degree, but what good was it when I spent the next 10 years managing strip joints and owning nightclubs? I looked and looked for a decent job, but Rent-a-Center was the only place that would hire me. It wasn't an ideal option, but it was the only option, so I took it. Suddenly, I found myself hawking electronics and furniture on layaway to the poorest people in the community. When they inevitably started to miss payments, I was the one that had to go into the projects and try to repossess the TV or Xbox - sometimes the people would try to physically fight me. It was bad, but things were about to get worse.

Around this time, I started to hear whispers from people around town that claimed Ian owed them money. It was the first red flag I had encountered since the Big Sean party - from my perspective, Ian's business was a wild success, and he had continued that success when he took over Tuxedo Junction - and I shrugged it off at first. You can't always believe everything you hear, and I gave Ian the benefit of the doubt. In a business like his that relies on small private investments and has to survive the highs and lows of the nightclub industry, disputes are bound to happen. Then those whispers became louder and more frequent - I came to understand that he owed some serious people some serious money, and began to suspect that the problems ran much deeper. I wish I had investigated more fully at the first signs of these problems, but as much as it was my business, it wasn't really my business, and I stayed out of it for as long as I could.

Suddenly, the monthly checks that Ian was sending me for use of the liquor license stopped coming in. I didn't care to get into it with him - I was busy with my own shit, working full time at Rent-a-Center and dealing with a lot of other personal matters. All I knew was that money that was owed to my family wasn't being paid, and that was enough for me to do something drastic. I pulled the license, forcing Ian to either shut down completely or continue to operate illegally without a valid liquor license. Foolishly, he chose the latter, another example of his childish belief that everything would work itself out if he just continued pushing forward. What none of us knew at the time was that this would be the straw that broke the camel's back.

Then the calls from FBI agents started to come in - to my cell phone, to my house, to my mother's house, even to work. They always wanted to know about my dealings with Ian - how did I know him, what kind of money did we make together and what did I know about his business? I gave non-answers and avoided the incessant calls as best I could as I tried to figure out what the fuck was going on. Al was getting the calls as well, only more so and with more intensity, as he had been working more and more directly with Ian as I had distanced myself from them. Together, we took the minor details we had managed to get from the FBI agents and everything else we had observed and heard over the last few years and started to put the pieces together. We had always known that Ian managed to secure invest-ments from locals in his party business. We even had begun to realize that he might be in some kind of trouble that he was hiding from us. But it wasn't until the FBI investigation really started to heat up that the full picture became clear, and it was outright terrifying.

After the Big Sean concert failed, Ian found himself with a big problem. He had taken tens of thousands of dollars from investors to cover the expenses for the event, but when the smoke cleared, he didn't have enough to repay even their initial investments, let alone the larger return he had promised them. Instead of scaling back and repaying them gradually through smaller events, as we suggested he do, he sought out even bigger investments from new people, and used those to pay back his initial investors as well as throw more parties and fund his increasingly lavish lifestyle. This cycle continued as he tried to brush it off and push forward, accumulating more debt, which required increasingly larger investments to pay off, and on and on until he owed so many people so much money that it became impossible for him to cover his bases. As he became more and more desperate, he started to guarantee a 15, 20% return on investments, unheard of in any kind of business, but his public track record of success and his minor celebrity had allowed him to gain the trust of serious investors. When he failed to keep his promises, those serious investors started to talk to serious individuals in law enforcement, who started to poke around and discover just how deep it all ran.

For two years, Ian had been robbing Peter to pay Paul - otherwise known as running a Ponzi scheme. It didn't help that he had also been extremely careless in handling his money. When you're a kid, you can get away with making relatively small money under the table and putting it through your bank. But not if you're dealing with hundreds of thousands of dollars, and possibly even millions of dollars like Ian was. He was depositing money from one investor into his bank account, and immediately wiring money to another investor from the same account, without ever being able to show any kind of legitimate income. And when he stopped being able to do that, he started to write checks and immediately close the account so the checks would bounce, in some ridiculous, hope-less attempt to buy himself a little more time. Ian's dad was a chef - he didn't know anything about handling a lot of money like my parents and Al had taught me to. And he ignored all of our advice about how to protect himself - another example of his immature belief that everything would be ok.

Add his flashy, public persona and personal spending on top of it all, the FBI agents that were working the case had probably never had it so easy. Ian continuing to open Tuxedo Junction after I pulled the liquor license only added to the heat that was already on him and raised more red flags at more law enforcement agencies, triggering a full investigation into Ian and all of his associates - including me. But they don't come out and tell you that you're being investigated. That's now how it works. They start with the phone calls, which only become more frequent and intrusive as you try to avoid them. Then they visit you at home and at work, always calm but threatening, always popping in, trying to jam you up, trying to make your life difficult. I kept things vague - the truth was, I didn't really know much - but they kept grilling me. Even if they're not charging you with anything, they keep hounding you in the hope that you'll want to snitch just to put an end to it all. Before long, I was fired from Rent-a-Center due to the constant calls and visits from FBI agents. They didn't want to deal with the daily annoyances that come with an investigation into one of their employees - it's hard to blame them.

It was a stressful time. None of us knew the details of the case, or when the hammer would fall and on who. I feared being arrested myself, and scrambled to put the few assets I still had in my name under my mother's so that they couldn't be seized. I decided that I would try to do anything I could to save us in the final hour. I discovered that the FBI would only be able to charge Ian with crimes related to investments from the individuals that they were working with, and any investments Ian had received from those that stayed away from the investigation, for all intents and purposes, fell outside the purview of the FBI. In other words, even if they looked into Ian's bank records and saw that he illegitimately put a million dollars through Wells Fargo, the scope of their investigation into the most serious felonies was limited to the money that came from investors that were cooperating. Without the information and testimony they would provide, the charges against Ian would be relatively minor and the major crisis would be averted.

I reasoned that if I could find a way to get those people their money back, or at least strike some kind of deal that would make them happy, they might give Ian a break, decide an entire criminal case would be more trouble than it was worth, and stop cooperating. I made some phone calls and learned that at that point in the investigation, the amount of money Ian owed to those individuals working with the FBI was $200,000. I didn't have that kind of liquid cash on hand, but I had another idea. I offered to put my condo up as collateral, hoping that it might be enough to appease Ian's investors and buy him some time to pay him back. For whatever reason, that deal never materialized, and not long after, Ian was arrested.

CHAPTER 21

It soon became clear that Al and I were safe from being arrested ourselves, but I was a mess. Everything I had built was crashing down around me. I was fortunate to have distanced myself from Ian and Tuxedo Junction, and my name was absent from the many news articles that started popping up, but people around town knew I was involved. Once again, I felt like a loser, and that I had failed to live up to my potential as the son of upstanding, respectable people like my parents. I thought I found my purpose at Club Lush and Tuxedo, and spent my twenties and early 30s trying to fully realize that purpose, only for it to be torn from my hands. It probably goes without saying that both clubs were shut down after Ian's arrest. I had nowhere to turn. I was out of work for a while, and fell into a deep depression amidst the chaos. My brother Mike had closed down his gym and moved to South Carolina a few years earlier, and my mother convinced him to come home to help me and our family through the difficult time. We moved into a humble townhouse in New Britain, and together we built up a routine that helped me get my mindset back on track. We worked out and even got into boxing, which became an outlet for my mind and body.

I got another day job, this time selling car parts at Autozone, to keep myself busy while I laid low as the investigation played out. It took time, but eventually, in January of 2015, Ian was indicted on charges of mail fraud, money laundering and making false statements - serious federal crimes that you'd expect a mobster to face, not a 20 year old kid. The trial was scheduled for the following Fall, and I continued working at Autozone and even got a side hustle selling energy over the phone as I waited for the hammer to drop. I was able to avoid being subpoenaed, but Al wasn't so lucky. When the trial started in October, he was called on to testify in court. Ultimately, it only lasted a month - it was an open and shut case - and in November of 2015, Ian was convicted on several of the charges. I managed to stay out of serious trouble, but I was one of the people that got hit the hardest when all was said and done. In October of the following year, after

Ian was sentenced to 3 years in federal prison, the town took over ownership of Tuxedo Junction and Club Lush, and we were forced to walk away. I didn't even get any of my money back.

Ian, the clubs, the money, the lifestyle - it was all in the past now. The saga was over - the rise and fall completed in a tragic fashion. But I had to push forward. After leaving Autozone, I was able to get a job as a union roofer, installing roofing at construction sites in the area for a decent, honest paycheck. In some ways, it was a relief. I didn't have to worry about liability, liquor licenses, rappers, hundreds of thousands of dollars, FBI investigations, whole teams of staff, any of the constant stresses of owning nightclubs. All I had to do was wake up, go to work, do what I was told, and go home. But with difficult, strenuous manual labor came physical stress, stress to my body - my muscles, my back, my bones. That job beat the shit out of me, and it started to take its toll on my body early. I wasn't the young man in peak physical condition that I once was - I was getting into my mid-30's, and was waking up with pains and aches on a daily basis.

The damage to my ego was even more difficult to manage. When I owned Tuxedo Junction and Club Lush, I was a superstar, a king. Guys wanted to be me, girls wanted to fuck me, and every day was a nonstop party. It was crazy, and dangerous, but it was fun, and I was in charge. I was the man. But by the time I was roofing, I had faded into the crowd and become a regular guy, something I had never been before. Part of this was deliberate. I was desperate to get back into the game, to start a new business, to make my big comeback, but my mother and brother urged me to continue to lay low. They were right - I had to bide my time until I could completely shed the legal heat and unwanted attention I had on my back as a result of my dealings with Ian. As much as it went against everything in me, it was a necessity to fade away and become indistinguishable - just an average Joe, installing roofing, working an honest job.

Still, the hustle didn't stop. Even as I worked a job as stable and boring as roofing, I was always looking for another angle, another opportunity to fill my pockets. Every day, all of the workers on the site would get together and order lunch from the same place - one guy would take the orders and money and pick up the food for everyone. I noticed that guys would often be short on lunch money and have to borrow it from each other, either because they didn't have the cash on them, or because they didn't have it at all until payday. One day, one of them asked me to spot him the five dollars he needed for a sandwich, and a lightbulb went off in my head. The following morning, I made sure to bring enough cash to cover lunch for the whole crew, and volunteered to be the one to order for everyone. As I expected, some of the guys were short. I happily offered to pay for their lunch, as long as they paid me back - with a couple dollars interest for the trouble. Just like that, I had a new side hustle as a miniature loan shark. You might not think a few dollars here and there is much, but it adds up - we're talking about 15, 20 guys, 5 days per week.

My business model was so good that it started to get awkward between myself and some of my coworkers that were late on paying me back, and I had to be careful with how I dealt with them. I knew that everyone got paid on Fridays, and that was the day that I started to talk to them a little more sternly. I knew they were waiting on their check to repay their debt, but wouldn't have the money on-hand until they cashed it out after they clocked out for the day. They'd ask if they could pay me back the following day, on Saturday, and I told them that was fine, I would be able to pick it up, but only if they added on a few extra dollars. More often than not, they'd say yes, and that's how I'd spend my Saturdays - making the rounds to all the guys' houses and picking up the money they owed me, usually a few hundred dollars in total. Not bad at all.

This was the hustle mindset that had always been inside me, since I was selling those one dollar candy bars from my flag football team for five dollars a piece, and it was still with me even as I installed roofing all those years later. I was able to utilize that part of me somewhat by loaning out lunch money, but it would never fully satisfy the urges I had for more and greater things for myself. A life of manual labor was not for me - I wasn't improving myself, I wasn't learning anything, I wasn't creating anything or applying myself fully. The only thing I got was the ability to install a roof. And the physical toll that the work was taking only increased. On multiple occasions, it got so hot up there that I passed out from heat exhaustion. This was on top of all the other ways it was killing my body. After about a year of roofing, I gave it up.

That decision was made even easier by a new opportunity that presented itself. Through a friend, I was able to get a daily route driving a box truck, delivering a load from Bristol, Connecticut down to New Jersey and back. It was easy, honest work that paid well, and I developed an interest in the business. Over the course of my first year in this new field, I learned about things like maintenance, how to get new clients, the different kinds of trucks, the finances - all the ins and outs. It sparked that hustler's, businessman's mindset within me, and before long I had a box truck of my own, and partnered up with one of my closest friends to start a business. We quickly and easily accumulated contracts with several local companies, and real money started to come in. In some ways, I was finally back.

CHAPTER 22

Around this time, my mother's health began to decline. She knew that she was getting older and wouldn't be around forever, and needed to get her various affairs in order in case, God forbid, anything might happen - we called it an exit strategy. These were extremely complex matters. It wasn't the average situation where someone owns maybe a house and certain possessions and some modest amount of liquid cash, and a will is written up to distribute everything amongst their loved ones in the case of their passing. My parents were very successful, wealthy individuals, and had many different financial interests - real estate, stocks, businesses, trusts, investments - all of which had to be dealt with. It wasn't as simple as who gets what - these interests had to be carefully managed, and it had to be determined who would be the one to take that responsibility, and what exactly that might entail. As far back as I can remember, she was always the one in charge of the money, and she was incredibly knowledgeable when it came to all financial matters. She had expertly managed the family's investments and built an impressive portfolio over the years. She was in total control - that was how she liked it, and it had always worked well for her. But now she was faced with the realization that certain things weren't in her control, and that she might even have to relinquish some of it while she was still here, and it was an extremely difficult pill for her to swallow.

It's not that she didn't believe in me. But after everything that had happened with the clubs, with Ian, she was concerned about my future, and whether I could step up and be the one to continue to build on everything she had worked for her whole life. We had many difficult conversations, even fights, about the direction that things should go in. Eventually, she let me take on more of a role in the handling of our investments, and soon I was present on phone calls with the various investment companies she was involved with and helping her set long term goals, structure deals, and even move money around.

About a year after I started my own box trucking

business, business was booming. I had fully transitioned into a new phase of my life, and successfully built another company from the ground up. I was already starting to think about what my next move would be. Old feelings were resurfacing, desires I had suppressed for years but had never fully left me. Box trucking was solid work, and I was having success with it, but it was boring. I missed the excitement of the nightlife industry, the lights, the music, the party. I missed the feeling of being a superstar, of taking risks, of making deals. But it wasn't a return to nightclub ownership that was calling to me - it was something more. I had been through so many crazy things in my life, and I was reaching a place where I finally wanted to share them with the world. Ideas for movies, TV shows and podcasts filled my head - I knew that I had a lot to offer, and I wanted a platform that would allow me to reach people. I started to do research and take meetings as those ideas became more fully formed. Then the pandemic hit. Fortunately, we continued getting steady box trucking work - if anything, there was an increased demand for our services as the supply-chain faltered in the face of COVID - but my dreams were put on hold. Throughout the Summer of 2020, I was driving the truck almost every day.

One day, in September of 2020, I was out on a

route with my partner when I received a phone call from my brother Mike. I could hear my mother's pained cries in the background as Mike told me, in a panic, that she fell down and he didn't know what to do. I told him to physically pick her up and take her to the hospital himself, immediately. They were at our family vacation house in New Hampshire along with my oldest son, so my partner dropped me off at my house, continued the route with his son, and I drove straight to the hospital as fast as I possibly could. When I arrived, my mother was in and out of consciousness, and the doctors told me they were preparing her for an MRI that would allow them to see what the problem was. Ultimately, she was diagnosed with a severe infection in her small intestine, and we were informed that immediate, emergency surgery would be needed to save her life.

The doctors worked late into the night, then gave us the good and bad news - the surgery had been a success, but my mother was in such bad shape, and her vitals signs were so low, it would be too dangerous for them to stitch her back up until her condition improved. As the oldest child, the doctors needed my approval to put her into an induced coma in the hopes that she would regain enough strength to allow them to finish the job. I gave the OK, and the next day

I was allowed to visit her. It was a difficult sight to behold - my mother, unconscious, her insides exposed with only a thin white sheet covering her as she lay there. It was made all the more painful by the uncanny similarities to what we had been through with my father. We were totally powerless - all we could do was hope, pray, and agonizingly wait. Unfortunately, the result would be the same as well. Less than a week had passed since I received that phone call from Mike when doctors informed me that my mother's condition would not improve enough to bring her back to full health. They could keep her alive in her current state, but she would never be anything more than a vegetable.

Yet again, the decision fell on my shoulders. With my father, my mother was technically the person that had to make the call, but she had given me the responsibility while she dealt with the immediate shock of his sudden fall into illness. Now it was just me. Mike was in shock himself - he didn't know what to do. But I had to act. I knew my mother would never want to live in that state, and that there was no way she would ever really come back to us. So after a few days of thinking, I made the decision to pull the plug, and we prepared to say our goodbyes. My son Julian had been so upset after witnessing his grandmother's fall, that he hadn't gone to the hospital to visit her. I couldn't blame him - he was very, very close with my mother, and it would have been unbearable for him to see her in that condition. He was 12 years old at that point, still a kid, but I was honest with him about the situation. I told him that grandma was very sick, and she wasn't getting better, and that the doctors and I decided it would be best to let her pass. This upset him even more, and even angered him. He was too young to really understand - all he heard was that I was killing grandma - and for a long time, he blamed me for her passing.

When the time came, Julian stayed at the house, and my brother and I went to see our mother for the last time. We held her hands and said our goodbyes as she took her last breath. And just like that, she was gone, less than a week after the first signs of serious illness. And again I had been forced to pull the plug - it felt unfair that I was put into that position not just with one parent, but two. At least I had been able to save my father's life on that first night, to give him another chance, to give him his last breaths, a last expression of my love. But with my mother, it was over before I even got to New Hampshire. And it had come after two years of us being at odds over our family affairs and the direction my life was taking. I spent my life trying to prove myself to her, to live up to the example that she and my father set, to make her proud, and suddenly she was taken from me in the middle of a low point in our relationship. I didn't get to say goodbye, I didn't get to apologize for the stress I caused her or for all of our fights over the years. I was heartbroken, and I was lost.

CHAPTER 23

My mother was the sergeant in our family - she was in charge, and she kept everything in order. She was a powerful presence, and she had steered all of us in the right direction over the years. She was successful in everything she had ever done - she had PHD's, she had taken our families investment portfolio into the millions, she raised two orphans from Colombia into good men under her roof. Her knowledge was top tier - anything you had a question about, she had the answer. Now those answers were gone, and the questions were piling up. What would I do without her? I had become more involved in our family's affairs over the years, but even up until her passing she was the one that called the shots. I was faced with the daunting prospect of navigating a complex web of properties, investments, stocks, trusts and attorneys all on my own. But first, I had to mourn.

I spent two weeks recovering from the shock of losing my mother so suddenly. She was cremated, and she wanted no funeral, not even a small service. My brother and I shared the somber responsibility of notifying friends and family members of what happened. In the wake of her death, I spent many hours thinking about our relationship, the good and the bad. The irony was, the elements of her personality that caused us to clash over the years were the same ones she instilled in me. Confidence, intelligence, mental strength, stubbornness, a constant drive to action - so many of the things that make me who I am, I got from her. What pained me the most was that I felt that I never really showed that to her in the way I wanted to. Part of the reason I pushed so hard to have more say in our family affairs was my desire to prove myself to her. If I was able to build on her life's work while she was still around to see it, it would have been the ultimate sign of appreciation for everything she had done for me. It would have been my way of telling her that she had done good, that her legacy would live on, that, despite our physical differences and our fights over the years, deep down I really was like her, and I was proud of it, and I wanted her to be proud of it too. And I thought if I had the chance, she really would be. But that chance was taken from me, and it hurt me deeply.

That pain would have crippled other people - they would have let it fester, multiply, spread and strengthen - but not me. That's not how I was raised. As the shock wore off, the hurt and regret became motivation and determination. After those two weeks, I was ready to take on the many burdens of settling our family business. The fact that I hadn't been able to prove myself to my parents while they were still alive only strengthened my resolve. Fortunately, I wouldn't be completely alone. My brother and I had become closer over the few years leading up to this point, and my mother's death only brought us closer. We were going to do it together, in our way. As family. First we had to take care of the simple things. Prior to her passing, my mother was still teaching part time at Southern. We had to notify the school of her death, and head down to the office she still kept there to remove her belongings. I remember packing up her things and looking around at the many prestigious diplomas, awards and honors hung on the walls. It was another opportunity to marvel at all of her accomplishments, and I realized again how lucky I was to have been raised by such an incredible woman.

In the case of a valuable, complex estate like my mother's, involving many distinct assets, it is an extremely time-consuming and complicated process to sort everything out. It's not just about splitting up the money - the money was tied up in different trusts, different accounts, properties, stocks, businesses, handled by investment companies and lawyers and bankers that were mostly strangers to us. Ensuring the equitable distribution of those assets would require working directly with those individuals, all while trying to make sense of the bigger picture and the advanced, minute details. You might think these people are there to help you understand, and that their incentives align with your own. But they're not working for you - they're working for the estate, an important distinction that I learned the hard way early on. There were a series of attorneys involved, each with their own specialty - an estate attorney, a trust attorney, a family attorney - none of whom I had a real prior relationship with. There is a lot of overlap between their responsibilities, and all parties involved seemed to have their hands on everything. This created a seemingly impenetrable barrier between my family and what was owed to us. But as time passed, as we got to know them and understand exactly what they were supposed to be doing, we realized who we would be able to trust, and who we wouldn't.

I started to receive letters notifying me that the mortgage on one of our family properties had gone unpaid for some months, and that it was in danger of going into foreclosure. I discovered our trust attorney was responsible for managing this property, and I scheduled a meeting between him and my brother and I. As soon as we walked into his expensive office, I knew he was going to be a problem. This guy handled tens of millions of dollars for some of the wealthiest families in Connecticut - his firm handled hundreds of millions. The way he looked at my brother and I, two Hispanic guys, told me everything I needed to know. Just because we looked and acted differently than his other clients, he didn't take us seriously, and it almost seemed like he was suspicious of us - he didn't think we could handle affairs. This was despite the fact that he was the one that was fucking up, and his laziness and poor management was hurting our family. He shrugged off our concerns - I felt disrespected, and I knew we had to get rid of him.

We didn't have the power to fire him. We would have to build up a case, and file a lawsuit to have him removed from his position, an extremely difficult process that I was advised against pursuing. I had the disadvantage in this battle - he knew money, he knew how to play the game, he knew all the ins and outs of this world that I was just starting to learn about. But I knew what was best for my family, and I wouldn't be intimidated. I began to build my case against him, and at the same time figure out how to prevent our property from going into foreclosure. Though my brother was by my side, I felt alone. I didn't know anyone that understood the complexities involved in multi-million dollar affairs. My mother was always the one that handled those things. I wished that I had spent more time learning from her, but I hadn't. I needed guidance, and I had to find it from someone else, someone that I could trust.

I turned to an old friend, my former partner Al, who had always been a great source of knowledge. He agreed that it would be almost impossible to build enough of a case against the trust attorney to have him removed, but he gave helpful advice on how I should proceed in the effort. As far as my attempt at preventing the property from going into foreclosure, Al didn't think I had any options, and advised me to let it play out. In a situation like this, it's not like paying rent - every one of these assets is tied together, every dollar accounted for, each a piece of a puzzle that must be kept in place so that the entire picture remains clear. If money from one account is taken out to pay the back-mortgage and late fees, that could trigger problems elsewhere. Though I respected Al as much as any man I had ever met, I disagreed - I didn't want to suffer the consequences of the trust attorney's mistakes. My brother and I went into our own pockets to pay what was owed on the house, at a time when we weren't exactly rich, and when everyone around told us that it would be a bad idea.

I spent 8 grueling, stressful months building our case against the trust attorney, countless hours pouring over countless pages of paperwork and compiling everything together. Finally, I was ready to take him on. I scheduled another meeting with him - this time, I walked into his expensive office with confidence, and I looked him right in his high-priced face and recited the case I spent the better part of a year building. He didn't want to lose our account - it would amount to him losing hundreds of thousands of dollars - but I watched his smirk slowly turn into a shocked grimace as he began to understand that I had him beat. He fucked up, and I caught him. He had no choice but to step down. Next time someone that looks like me walks into his office, maybe he'll treat them better.

Once that was taken care of, my brother and I hired a trustee that wasn't an attorney to take care of our family's various trusts, and we also hired an attorney to represent our own interests separate from those of the estate. Now it was a matter of dividing everything up between my brother and I, a process that would take years. Mike didn't get along with the estate attorney, and had difficulty working with him, which gave me the opportunity to take charge. I knew how I wanted to set things up for myself as well as my kids and future grandkids, and I did everything I could to move things forward in a way that aligned with my plan. I worked directly with my brother to decide which one of us would get what assets. As anyone might expect, we butted heads many times during the process. During one particularly contentious disagreement, I was even advised to get my own attorney to go against Mike - thankfully, we were able to avoid escalating the conflict to that level. Even when we had a verbal agreement on any individual matter, the ensuing paperwork required to make it official took months. It was stressful, time-consuming, and complicated, but I knew how important it was to get it right.

CHAPTER 24

All in all, it took three years of going back and forth with my brother and fighting attorneys to get things settled in the way I wanted - even as I write this in 2023, we are still ironing out the final details. Mike has his share to use as he wants, and mine is carefully arranged in a collection of assets that I carefully chose to ensure my kids and even theirs are taken care of. Still, there was more work to be done. One of those assets was the house I bought for my mother in Fairfield, which needed to be sold. I was also going to be moving into a bigger house myself, and needed to sell my own house in Southington. In the past, I would have hired someone to take care of it for me - this time, I took charge myself. Renovations needed to be done, so I hired a few friends and we got to work. When the houses were ready to be put on the market, I listed them myself. When I found buyers, I wrote up the deals and collected the funds all on my own. It was a sign of a transformation that had been taking place, one that I had been unaware of until that point.

I was so preoccupied during the few years following my mother's passing that I didn't realize what exactly was going on inside me, how I was changing, growing, and learning. Even during the most successful times of my life, I lacked a certain element that makes for a truly accomplished person, like my mother, my father or Al - foresight. When I was in the nightclub business, all I ever thought about was what was going on that minute, that day, that week, that month, and it worked for me, I did big things, but I never considered what would be happening 10 years down the road. I succeeded in the short term, but failed in the long term, and as a result, had not been able to fully establish myself or reach my full potential. Spending all that time sorting through my mother's life work, learning the ins and outs of dealing with millions of dollars, collaborating with investment firms, bankers and attorneys, all of it helped me understand what it takes to build and sustain the kind of generational wealth I wanted for my family. Patience, knowledge, hard work, meticulous planning - these were the parts of my mindset that had been lacking. But no more. I had always known what I wanted - finally I knew how to get it. I see now that on the day my mother died, I became a monster - in business, in finance, in taking care of my family, and in turning my biggest dreams into reality.

When I closed on both of the properties I was selling, I was left with more liquid cash than I had ever had before. Together, those transactions amounted to nearly two million dollars in my pocket - these were the kinds of deals I always dreamed about making, the kinds of deals that guys like Al and Mike did, the kinds of deals that set a guy like me up for something huge. With my sons' futures taken care of, it was finally time to pursue my latest dream and enter into a new industry. I had stories to tell, and I wanted to reach and inspire people, but I needed a platform. Now I had the money to make one myself. I started a podcast, "Parental Vision", showcasing parents and their stories of struggle and perseverance. I self-funded a pilot for a reality show called "Single Fathers", highlighting the lives of single fathers like myself. All of this was accomplished with the help of young men and women from the community that I hand-picked to be a part of something special that I was building, people that otherwise wouldn't have had a chance at a career in media and entertainment because of the way they look. With them on my side, I know that anything is possible.

I have movies, books and more TV shows in the works - I'm even getting into acting. If it interests me, if I feel like I have something to offer or more to give, I go for it. It's a new phase of my life - Big Steve, the multi-millionaire, the entertainment mogul. Who would have predicted that? Old friends often ask why the Hell I bother. They tell me that if they were in my shoes, they would retire, get a vacation home and live off the millions for the rest of their life without ever lifting a finger again. Why don't I do that? If you've read this far, you probably have a good idea. If I had even a little bit of that mindset within me, I never would have gotten to the position I'm in now. This new stage of my life doesn't tell me that it's time to pack it in - it only inspires me to push harder. To me, it's just an opportunity to move onward and upward, a springboard that will deliver me to the next phase, which will lift me up to the next one and that one to the next after that.

What is it that makes me the man I am today? What is it exactly that allowed me to transcend, to successfully traverse the difficult path from orphan to millionaire? When I think about where I came from and the odds that were stacked against me, sometimes it feels like it was fate that I would become truly successful. But deep down, I know fate had nothing to do with it. It was things like hard work, life experience and knowledge that put me into the position I'm in now. Two wonderful parents to teach me the ways of the world and show me my potential, along with friends and business partners that helped guide me along the way. And more than anything, it was that hustle mindset that was always inside me, that remains today and always will.

Through all of the ups and downs I experienced in my life, it was the hustle that kept me moving forward and prevented me from ever giving up. I was always looking for a new angle, a new venture, I always had a new idea, I always saw potential in places others didn't. I have changed and learned so much over the years, had many failures and many successes, been the superstar and the bum more times than I can count. But the hustle was always there. When I was selling candy bars and lighters, when I was loaning lunch money, when I managed strip clubs and owned nightclubs, at Rent-A-Center, at Sherwin Williams, at Autozone, in business class when I invented pizza sticks. The hustle was always there. My parents knew about education, business, finance, and so did Al. My friends knew the streets, how to work them and how to make money. But no one had been through it all and come out on top like I had. So where did it come from? What is it that embedded the hustle deep within me?

As I looked at my collection of sneakers on the day that I decided to write this book, I began to reflect on those very questions. In many ways, shoes themselves are a symbol of my journey. I thought about the blood-soaked shoes I wore as I ran from my childhood home. I thought of my sore, bare feet and the shoes I coveted at the orphanage. I thought of the pair they gave me on the day my parents picked me up. I thought of the Jordan's I wore to school as a child and the way they caused me to stand out amongst the white kids in Sperry's. I thought of the different pairs I collected and wore over the years across the many different phases of my life. I knew that it was my attachment to sneakers that could give me the answer I was looking for, but nothing clicked. I reflected for hours, searching within myself. Suddenly, night had fallen, and I realized it was time to say goodnight to Julian and go to sleep myself.

As I opened the door to his room, I caught a glimpse of his own Jordans sitting there on the floor in front of his bed, a habit he inherited from his father. At that moment, something became clear to me. I thought of the origins of this odd family tradition. It all goes back to my first few weeks in America, when I wore my sneakers to bed out of the fear that if

I took them off, they wouldn't be there when I woke up. Eventually, my parents reassured me to the point that I was comfortable taking them off, but not enough that I would let them out of sight. I didn't want to go back to being the boy without shoes - I couldn't, and I wouldn't. It wasn't fear - I had been through things most grown men only see on TV, I wasn't scared of anything. It was a powerful instinct to survive that caused me to hold tight the shoes, and the pillows and the blankets and the toys and the food, all of the things that represented my separation from my bleak life in Columbia and a future of certain doom.

I realized then, standing there in Julian's room, where the hustle came from. It didn't appear out of thin air, it wasn't given to me and it wasn't taught. It evolved out of that survival instinct, the silver lining running through my violent childhood, the gift and the curse I received the day bullets rained down upon my home and which strengthened within me as I traversed the desolate hellscape of the orphanage. When I arrived in America, these instincts were vigorous but basic, like something from an anthropological book about early humans. I knew that I needed food in my stomach, a shirt on my back, a roof over my head - I was desperate to hold onto everything I got, and I knew that the more I had, the less likely it was that it could be taken away. This explains my compulsive, early stealing habit.

As I got older and came to understand the American way and the American dream, I learned that there was more to life than mere survival. I saw first-hand the chasmic gap between the lives of successful people like my parents and those of the people that were just getting by. I learned the value of money, of knowledge, of being financially comfortable and protected, of being able to truly provide for your family. My mother and father set the example - through them, I was able to identify the kind of man I wanted to be. That is when that survival instinct evolved into the hustle, the unwavering drive not simply to survive in this crazy world, but to thrive.

All of that isn't to say that coming out of a traumatic childhood is the only key to success, and of course it isn't any kind of guarantee. In my case, my difficult background imbued me with a particularly powerful and ingrained hustle from an early age, and it was essential to my journey. But the hustle can be adopted by anyone, at any time - it's never too late. And the hustle mindset is only one element of the overall psychology of success, one piece of the puzzle that I have spent my life solving and that I am still gathering all of the pieces to. It took many years, many ups and many downs for me to put it all together. When I was younger, I had the hustle, I had the immediacy and the energy, and I found success, but I didn't have the longevity or the foresight. I was satisfied too easily, I took it all for granted, and because of that, I let everything slip out of reach. I had to learn how to hold on.

These days, I treat my successes like I treat my Jordans - never let them too far out of sight, and always be on the lookout for more. And that's what I'm going for now, just like I always have - more. I hope that I have been able to inspire you in your own journey, wherever you may come from and wherever you may be headed. I hope that this book can be one small piece of your puzzle, one small step towards your own dreams. And more than anything, I hope that one day, we can meet each other on top. - Big Steve

ABOUT THE AUTHOR

Big Steve Prohaska is an entrepreneur, business owner, and the mind behind the growing multi-media platform Parental Vision. He is also the creator and host of the groundbreaking, upcoming reality series Single Fathers.

To learn more about Steve, visit parental-vision.com.

facebook.com/stephen.prohaska

instagram.com/bigstevebigmoves